If Grace Is So Amazing, Why Don't We Like It?

Donald McCullough

JOSSEY-BASS
A Wiley Imprint
www.josseybass.com

Published by Jossey-Bass
A Wiley Imprint
989 Market Street, San Francisco, CA 94103-1741 www.josseybass.com

Jossey-Bass books and products are available through most bookstores. To contact Jossey-Bass directly call our Customer Care Department within the U.S. at 800-956-7739, outside the U.S. at 317-572-3986, or fax 317-572-4002.

Jossey-Bass also publishes its books in a variety of electronic formats. Some content that appears in print may not be available in electronic books.

Library of Congress Cataloging-in-Publication Data

McCullough, Donald W., date.
If grace is so amazing, why don't we like it? / Donald McCullough.
p. cm.
Includes bibliographical references.
ISBN 0-7879-7437-4 (alk. paper)
1. Grace (Theology) I. Title.
BT761.3.M33 2005
234—dc22
2004025498

Printed in the United States of America
FIRST EDITION
HB Printing 10 9 8 7 6 5 4 3 2 1

Contents

Acknowledgments

CHIP MACGREGOR of Alive Communications deserves special recognition. He suggested I write about grace, encouraged me along the way, and used his considerable skills as a literary agent to find a good publishing home for it. I am grateful for his wisdom and friendship.

Julianna Gustafson was a joy to work with, an editor with a discerning eye, delightful wit, and gracious tact. What more could an author want? I am grateful, too, for the rest of the team at Jossey-Bass and the various ways they contributed to transforming my manuscript into a finished book.

My family—parents, children, stepchildren, in-laws, grandchildren (especially the grandchildren, whose existence witnesses to the prodigal love of God)—provided important support. Most of all, I thank God for my wife, Shari. Her friendship, partnership, support, and love mean more than I can express.

TO MY DAUGHTERS,

Jennifer Ziegler and Joy McCullough-Carranza,

with gratitude and great love

Part One

Upside Down

Chapter One

How Sweet the Sound?

It has been called America's most beloved song. We sing it in country churches and downtown cathedrals; we turn up the radio when we hear it belted out by pop vocalists or improvised by jazz ensembles; we lift lighted candles to it in dark stadiums and get a lump in the throat when bagpipes skirl it at funerals; we consistently name it as our favorite hymn. I refer, of course, to "Amazing Grace."

Let's be frank: we enjoy its balladlike melody, but its words are another matter. We're inspired by the way they were written—an eighteenth-century slave trader, John Newton, getting religion—but to the extent that we've paid any attention to them, we're likely to treat them with patronizing sentimentalism. They come from a different era. Today, who can sing with any real conviction "Amazing grace, how sweet the sound, that saved a wretch like me"? We might occasionally *feel* like a wretch, but we don't want anyone except our therapist to know. We've heard plenty of up-to-the-minute preachers, not to mention Oprah and Dr. Phil, assuring us that many of our problems stem from low self-esteem. Flagellating ourselves with guilt is unproductive. Sure, we make mistakes. Doesn't everyone? But we're adults here. None of this "wretch like me" stuff!

Grace set to music is one thing, but what about grace itself? What about grace as an idea? Grace as an act? Grace as a force?

We don't like it. It might be amazing, as the hymn insists, and it might be wonderful and marvelous and "a thought that changed the world" (as the band U2 sang on a recent album), and it might sometimes even be necessary, but when all the adjectives have worn themselves out with the hype and have called it a day, and we're left with nothing but the thing itself, then what? As I said, we don't like it.

To be sure, we appreciate brief encounters with it, such as when we forget to pay the health insurance premium and we're told not to worry because there is a "grace period," or when we've blown it and our spouse signals it's OK to quit the couch and return to bed, or when a friend whose feelings we've hurt invites us to lunch, or when an umpire calls a strike on a Yankee and even from the stands we could see the ball was closer to China than the strike zone, or when a policeman pulls us over for going ten miles over the limit and gives us a warning, or when we haul ourselves to church with a hangover and the preacher assures us that God forgives sins. At times like these we might sing "Amazing Grace" with a semblance of sincerity.

We're thankful for these minor reprieves, for Grace Lite. But if the real thing happens, if we're seized by a full-bodied, take-no-prisoners grace, we have far more ambivalent feelings. When a muscled arm of mercy lifts us by the scruff of the neck and sets us in a new place, a better place we neither earned nor deserved, we're likely to protest that, given time, we could have gotten ourselves there, thank you very much, and without the rough treatment.

Even worse, if grace happens to someone else, someone we *know* doesn't deserve it, someone we can't stand, then we don't want even to hear about grace, let alone see it in operation. In such circumstances, grace seems more like a miscarriage of justice.

Recall the last time you needed someone's forgiveness. Maybe you were angry with your husband, and you said something that lacerated him where he is most vulnerable. Immediately you knew it was wrong, terrible. You wanted to bite off your tongue. You said you were sorry, and the next day you sent flowers to his office, and that night you made his favorite meal. After dinner, when you tried to apologize once more, he wouldn't let you. He simply held you and said, "Forget it." The relief was wonderful. But I would bet part of my pension that, even with tears of gratitude flowing, you also heard a voice inside saying something like this: "Thank God he kept this in perspective. He knows I didn't really mean it, that I wasn't myself. He knows I'm not that kind of person, not really. He remembers my good qualities." In other words, you wanted the nasty incident put behind you and everything to be all right. But you didn't want grace, didn't want a *completely* undeserved gift.

Or maybe you cut the margins a little close at work and got the company up to its neck in IRS investigators. You had every reason to expect you would be fired. But when you found yourself on the other side of the boss's desk and felt sweat flowing down your back like the Columbia River, and you heard him say that after much consideration he would give you another chance, you were more than relieved, more than elated: you were being rescued from the morgue and given another chance at life. But unless I'm mistaken, before you got home that night and poured yourself a celebratory libation, you started thinking something like this: "Thank God they didn't make a big deal out of this. It was a stupid mistake. They're smart enough to see that at least I have a certain moxie, that I have the courage to risk failure, that I have skills too valuable to lose." In other words, you wanted to keep your job. But you didn't want grace, a *completely* undeserved gift.

Our instinctive reaction is to pull back from grace. We want to believe that, on balance, something in our lives merits the good that comes our way. We deserve whatever gifts we receive.

If we find it difficult to accept grace for ourselves, how much more unwilling are we to have it handed to others! When someone gets off the hook too easily, aren't you uncomfortable? When someone does something bad—steal money from a grandmother, say, or abuse an invalid, or commit a crime—don't you want that person to receive what's rightfully coming? Don't you have a primal, visceral instinct that wants others to get their just desserts? Don't you want wrongdoers to get the full measure of punishment they deserve, at least enough to make them really, really sorry? I mean, if you play by the rules (most of the time), and you see someone else breaking them, don't you want that person to be held accountable? Don't you want what's *fair?*

Well, grace is not fair. And that's the problem.

{ .. .. }

Imagine you have a younger brother who says he hopes the old man's two packs-a-day habit finally catches up with him because he can't wait for his inheritance. Imagine him so impatient that one day he begs your father to sell his stocks, downsize to a smaller home, and break into his retirement fund, so that he (the selfish brat) won't have to wait until the funeral is over and the estate has been liquidated. Imagine too that, for some inexplicable reason, your father accedes and gives him exactly what he wants, enabling your brother to hit the road for Vegas, where in a couple of weeks he blows the whole bundle on craps and booze and very expensive women.

Then your brother, after a few nights at the Union Gospel Mission, grows tired of the food and of getting "saved" at every altar call, and decides to return home—arriving at your father's new place, it turns out, the very day you've volunteered to repaint the rain gutters. Your father—you really can't believe your eyes—sees this miserable excuse of a son dragging his sorry backside down the sidewalk, and instead of waiting for him to make a convincing case for how bad he feels, runs out to meet him and throws his arms around him and laughs so loudly that neighbors open their front doors to see what's going on. Then your father—you really can't believe your ears—invites everyone to a party. Says he's going to have a BBQ. Wants everyone to wear their dancin' shoes.

Now, if you're anything like me, which against some evidence I maintain is near-normal, you'd be more than a little upset. I would climb down the ladder at a deliberate pace, pour the remaining paint into the can, wipe clean the outside of the can and firmly pound the lid in place, wash and shake dry the brushes—I would do a proper clean-up because I always do what needs to be done—and then I would get into my highly responsible Toyota and head for home. If my father called that afternoon to ask me to pick up a couple extra kegs for the party, I would do my best not to say what I was thinking, not to say this: "So this is what a guy has to do to get a party? He has to squander the family's wealth and be a selfish no-good playboy? Yes, I can imagine you must be relieved to know he's not lying in some gutter. But can't you see how this makes me feel? I've always been considerate, always tried to do more than was expected of me, always tried to make you proud. And you know, that's fine, that's who I am. I'm not complaining about that. But this son of yours . . . do you really think he deserves a welcome like this? What are you teaching him? That he can get away with this sort of thing?"

That evening I would pick up the kegs for him (forever a reliable son), but I can imagine myself lugging one up to the front door and hearing the raucous noise of the neighbors and the blaring band. And then, the final blow: looking in through the window and seeing my mother dancing on the dining room table. That would be more than I could take. I would drop the keg on the front lawn and get the hell out of there, driving into the darkness.

If this story sounds familiar, it's a loose paraphrase of an original you've no doubt heard many times. Jesus first told it. It's known as the parable of the prodigal son, which has always been a bad name for it because it's not about the young spendthrift, and not even about the loving father. It's really about you and me and our reaction to the father's grace. Jesus told the story in response to the grumbling of religious leaders, who were unhappy that he hung out with sinners and even partied with them. What sort of example would that set, anyway? Did he want scoundrels to get the wrong idea, to think God didn't care about immoral behavior, that they could flout God's laws? So Jesus told about a Father—the God who sent him—who loves so much he runs to wayward children to embrace them and throws a party in celebration of their return. This is who God is, Jesus said, *and this is who you are,* the oh-so-responsible elder siblings, refusing to come into the party, choosing rather to caress your high moral standards and slink away into the darkness of your own self-righteousness.

{ .. .. }

Well, it's hard to argue with Jesus.

But with all due respect, didn't the elder brother have a point? Isn't there at least a part of all of us that not only understands but sympathizes with him? He might have been a prig, but even prigs can sometimes be right. The truth is, grace that's not kept within reasonable limits *is* unfair. What sort of world would this be if standards were not upheld and laws could be broken with impunity? What sort of world would this be if unrestrained grace had its way?

How can we get around the fact that, according to Jesus, to understand God and God's relationship with the world we have to begin with grace? This is especially troublesome for Christians, who claim to follow the teaching of Jesus, but it is also problematic for those who consider Jesus simply a wonderful teacher. After all, this wasn't a minor part of the legacy he left us; this was its central theme. We can't fault him on this without negating his entire ministry.

But how can we go along with this, really? It would mean a total reversal of our values. It would disrupt everything. Absolutely everything.

What might work is this: don't reject grace, just tame it. Honor it, by all means, and enshrine it in official confessions and praise it in religious ceremonies, but keep it within reasonable bounds, keep it away from the rest of life, keep it from running wild. If grace remains free, it will get into too much mischief. So always qualify and explain it. Preach sermons about it, if you must, but always conclude with a mighty *therefore,* as in "therefore, this is what you must *do* in response to God's grace."

Karl Barth, the great Swiss theologian, said the most cunning strategy for defending ourselves against grace is to tame and harness it, to allow grace "to take its seat in the pew, cheerfully don the vestment and mount the pulpit, zealously to make Christian gestures and movements, soberly to produce theology, and in this way, consciously participating in the confession of Jesus Christ, radically to ensure that His prophetic work is halted, that it can do no more injury to itself, let alone to the world."[1]

So yes, sing "Amazing Grace" with gusto! Lift up your voice and hold hands with your neighbors and allow tears to flood your eyes and be assured that "When we've been there ten thousand years, / Bright shining as the sun, / We've no less days to sing God's praise / Than when we'd first begun."

For the time being, though, be careful: if grace slips out of the song and into your world, it will turn things upside down.

Chapter Two

Hanging on a Hair

WHY *WOULDN'T* WE protect ourselves against grace? Nothing has prepared us for it. In fact, we've been taught to expect the opposite. Our nurture, education, relationships, and cultural environment have conditioned us for antigrace.

Our world, we soon learn, runs according to an important law: if you desire a particular effect, you set in motion an appropriate cause. If you're hungry, you cry and your mother offers a breast. If you want to be held, you fuss and your father comes running in the middle of the night. If your diapers are full, you make funny faces and someone will change you. You're omnipotent (which is nice work if you can get it). But it doesn't last long. Eventually your mother and father decide, around 3:00 A.M., that you're not quite as cute as you once were and that they'd just as soon be asleep. They also want you to learn to do certain things for yourself. The important word in the last sentence is *do:* the law of cause and effect is not abrogated, only altered. As you grow older, you must master causes that become more varied and complicated. If you want the effect of a dry bottom, for example, there comes a time when crying no longer makes it happen and you have to learn a new cause; you have to hold the elimination of bodily wastes until you crawl up on the potty. When you first do this, you're rewarded not only with a clean bottom but also with wildly happy parents who offer you praise that is more sincere than you'll likely receive from them if in later years you happen to win the Nobel Prize.

A few weeks ago, my wife and I had just sat down to a wonderful candlelight dinner when the telephone rang. Normally, we would not have answered it, but Shari and I were expecting the birth of another grandchild and wanted to spring into action if the contractions had started. Shari held the receiver between us, so we could both hear the news at the same time, and what we heard, just as I put a fork full of savory salmon into my mouth was, "Grammy and Poppa, I just went poopie in the potty!" We congratulated our granddaughter, of course, and we encouraged her to keep up the good work.

Yes, *to keep up the good work,* because that's what she has to do to accomplish good things. To become a success in life, whether going to the bathroom or becoming the CEO of a major corporation, she will have to do the right work at the right time. If she fails she will have a mess to clean up, and if she succeeds she will have achievements to enjoy. *Keep up the good work, dear grandchild, because life demands work—long and hard and necessary work.*

Do you want to learn to play the piano? Take lessons and practice. Do you want to get into college? Study diligently in high school. Do you want to be wealthy? Put in long hours at the office. Do you want to be liked? Master attractive social skills. Do you want to be spiritual? Devote yourself to disciplines of piety.

If experience teaches anything, it is this: you must *earn* good things. Do you want something of value? Don't expect a miracle or handout. Rewards don't come to the lazy. You have to get off the couch and break a sweat; you have to roll up your sleeves and get your hands dirty.

Great symphonies and paintings and novels and poems and movies didn't fall from the sky. Someone went to considerable trouble to create them. And we enjoy them because we've learned to enjoy them, because we've expanded our knowledge to appreciate their complex treasures. And we have institutions of learning and health and government because countless others have dedicated their energy to building them, and we ourselves have continued the dedication by paying for their ongoing support.

Our nation was built on the conviction that when the going gets tough, as the saying goes, the tough get going. Gutsy emigrants had the can-do spirit to venture into the dangerous unknown of North America. Pioneers settled the west by crossing plains and climbing mountains and swimming rivers, and they arrived at places where they could . . . what? Rest? No, where they tilled soil and panned for gold and established ranches and built businesses. We followed them by laying railroad tracks and constructing highways, conquering diseases and reducing infant mortality, winning wars and establishing equitable laws, splitting the atom and walking on the moon.

We don't wait until things are given to us. That's why we're uneasy about anything that smacks of the welfare state. On the one hand, we want to defeat poverty; if there's a problem, we throw ourselves into the search for a solution, and one of the solutions we've tried is a safety net for the economically disadvantaged. But we're ambivalent about this; we're not sure it's the best approach. Some believe handouts only encourage idleness, which is only slightly worse than encouraging treason. After all, the law of cause and effect is still the law of the land, and if you want good things you had better earn them or quit your complaining; you had better put up or shut up.

{ .. .. }

That's why Jesus' parables are disconcerting.

Like the one about an owner of a vineyard who, sometime around October, sees his grapes are ripe and hears forecasters predicting an approaching cold front. He has to act, and fast. So the next morning at six o'clock he goes to wherever day laborers hang out—the union hall, maybe, or the local bar—and he agrees to a fair wage. He gets them started picking, but by nine he sees he will need more help. So he goes back to round up another busload. As the hours pass and the sky darkens, the vineyard seems larger than ever. He counts and calculates and concludes the grapes aren't going to get harvested without more help. Out he goes again—at noon, and again at three.

At five o'clock the situation is desperate. With only an hour left of picking, too many grapes remain. So—you guessed it—out he goes once more. You can imagine the sort of workers still there: tattoos everywhere, plenty of metal stuck through body parts, a carpet of cigarette butts and empty beer cans. But he has no choice. He tells them they're in luck, if they can stagger across the street to the bus and work for an hour.

Finally, the harvest is finished. By six every grape has been picked, and it's time to pay wages. The owner is jubilant. He tells his foreman, "Let's have some fun. Line 'em up, beginning with the last hired, and then the next-to-the-last, and so on."

When the beer brigade open their pay packets, they're stunned. A full day's wage! They had worked only an hour but were paid for twelve—proof that the gung-ho guys, so quick to jump on buses by dawn's early light, are idiots, proof that it's best to take it easy and let things run their course.

Those farther back in the line watch the laughter and backslapping, and they start their own celebrating, for surely those who worked longer will get pay packets that are fuller.

But no. Everyone receives the same amount, even the ones who started picking while dew was still on the grapes, who worked through scorching heat, who tore their hands and nearly broke their backs. As Robert Capon imagined it, this "goes down like Gatorade for the last bunch hired, like dishwater for the next-to-the-last, like vinegar for the almost-first, and like hot sulfuric acid for the first-of-all."[1]

When the latters' throats cool, they protest. "This is unfair! What do you think you're doing? Why would you pay those bums the same as us? They didn't work enough to moisten their armpits!"

The owner says, "Didn't I pay you the amount we agreed on—a fair wage? If I want to pay others more than they deserve, what's it to you? It's my money. Are you mad because I'm generous? Look, I'm about to break open a case of last year's reserve Cabernet, so why don't you sit down, have a drink, and enjoy the fun? Otherwise, get out of here so you don't spoil the party."

This is no way to run a business. I don't have an MBA, but I know that no one would do this sort of thing (except perhaps an Enron executive providing a sweet deal for his relatives).

This is also no way to run a religion. For God's sake, do you want to undermine the law of cause and effect? If you cast doubt on the importance of work, how will you motivate people to do what needs to be done? How will you get them to become more responsible, moral, and spiritual? What was Jesus thinking when he introduced this story by saying the Kingdom of Heaven is like this? What did he mean at the end of the story when he said, "So the last will be first, and the first will be last"?[2]

{ .. .. }

If we're not offended by the teaching of Jesus, we haven't really heard it. It's counterintuitive to our mind-set, our worldview, everything we've experienced. It's also alien to our culture; it cuts against the grain of our system of rewards and punishments. We can't help but be scandalized by it.

Jesus taught about another Kingdom: the reign of God. He claimed it was already present in him and would someday dawn in fullness. This Kingdom, I must stress, is wholly different, unlike anything already in this world. Jesus wasn't interested in adding a spiritual dimension to life as we know it. He didn't come to spiff things up, but to overturn them. The reign of God, as he taught it, overthrows all competing principalities and powers, all philosophies and systems. It does this for a disturbing, embarrassing, and shocking reason: it rests on grace.

So Jesus told outrageous stories about grace, and he acted out minidramas of grace—miracles of healing, in which the blind were given sight, the deaf were given hearing, the lame were given mobility, the dead were given life. *Were given:* they did not earn these things; they received them as gifts.

Not surprising, the first disciples of Jesus had difficulty grasping this. They were often as scandalized as his enemies. In fact, they didn't get it until after Good Friday and Easter. But it was precisely the disappointment of his death and the surprise of his resurrection that opened their eyes. Then they saw that what he had done (in his life) was fulfilled by all that had been done to him (in his death and resurrection). His ministry had been intensified, deepened, made even more scandalous; his message of grace had been confirmed as *the* universal truth. The authorities, in the name of law-abiding religion, had put him to death, and God had nonetheless raised him from the grave; it all confirmed that God's reign was nothing other than a reign of grace.

It turned everything upside down—for them and for us.

For the time being, there may be good reasons we must live in a world of cause and effect, where we must work to earn good things, and where we'll be punished if we fail. But we must understand that if the Christian faith is true, then this world as we know it, the world of law, is a temporary and doomed order. For if God has been revealed in Jesus Christ, as Christians maintain, then grace is the center of all reality. Grace is the heartbeat of the universe. Grace is the current in which all things flow.

The Bible, taken as a whole, is the unfolding story of grace: God creates the universe; God chooses Abraham and his descendents to be "a light to the nations"; God liberates Israel from Egyptian bondage; God stays committed to humanity through the triumphs and travails of the centuries until eventually, in the fullness of time, God sends Jesus the Messiah, who proclaims the good news of grace, getting himself killed in the process; and God, ever taking the initiative, ever working through the failures of this world, raises Jesus from death, and through that resurrection offers life to all.

Grace, then, whether we like it or not, is the central theme of the Christian faith. It is the innermost truth of all that will abide, the cause and goal of all things. This grace, when at last it takes hold of us and leaves us no choice but to acknowledge it, turns everything upside down.

G. K. Chesterton said that St. Francis, when he became a follower of Jesus Christ, had a radical change of perspective. His beloved Assisi, with its large masonry and massive foundations, its watchtowers and citadels, was upended:

> He might see and love every tile on the steep roofs or every bird on the battlements; but he would see

> them all in a new and divine light of eternal danger and dependence. Instead of being merely proud of his strong city because it could not be moved, he would be thankful to God Almighty that it had not been dropped; he would be thankful to God for not dropping the whole cosmos like a vast crystal to be shattered into falling stars. Perhaps St. Peter saw the world so, when he was crucified head-downwards.[3]

What St. Francis saw, Chesterton was saying, was that grace means that *nothing has to be.* Everything is a gift, not the result of human merit or work, and thus everything is dependent on God.

He who has seen the whole world hanging on the hair of the mercy of God has seen the truth; we might almost say the cold truth. He who has seen the vision of the city upside down has seen it the right way up.[4]

Part Two

Upside-Down God

Chapter Three

Surprising, Not Predictable

THE EASE WITH which we speak about God—and even *for* God—is remarkable: "God says . . . ," "God wills . . . ," "God told me . . . ," "God led me . . . ," "God showed me . . . ," "God bless America . . . ," "Oh, my God!" and of course the god-this and god-that phrases often used like punctuation. We blather on about deity as though we knew what we were talking about, as though we human beings have a perfect right to speak to and about and for the Almighty. Our ancestors might have dropped to their knees in God's presence, but we throw a palsy-walsy arm around God's shoulders. "The man upstairs," we say, not only in country songs but in ordinary conversation, despite the fact that God is not a man and not upstairs any more than downstairs, and we like this phrase, I think, because it implies that God is above all *familiar,* that God is like the guy renting the spare room—not exactly a member of the family, but not far away, easy enough to have around the house and to speak with occasionally and to call upon in emergencies.

“Why do people in churches seem like cheerful, brainless tourists on a packaged tour of the Absolute?” asks Annie Dillard. “Does anyone have the foggiest idea what sort of power we so blithely invoke?”[1]

Well, no, we don’t have the foggiest idea, because we *can’t* have the foggiest idea. God, as Søren Kierkegaard put it, is “qualitatively and infinitely other.” God is not “humanity” spoken in a loud voice. God is absolutely, essentially different—or to use the Bible’s word, holy.

When you encounter a God like this, according to those who have lived to tell about it, you don’t feel chummy; you feel awestruck, even terrified. When Moses heard God speaking out of the burning bush, he hid his face, afraid to look. When the Israelites received the Ten Commandments, they were told to stay back from Mt. Sinai unless they wanted to get fried. When Isaiah had a vision of God, he said, “Woe is me! I am lost!” When angels of the Lord announced the birth of Jesus—to Zechariah, to Mary, to Joseph, to the shepherds—they could not have even remotely resembled the cherubs adorning Christmas cards, for their first words always were, “Do not be afraid.” When Saul (later renamed Paul) encountered the resurrected Christ, he was thrown to the ground and blinded.

Evidently, meeting a Being who is qualitatively and infinitely other is more than a little unsettling, and dangerous. You should probably wear a helmet and an asbestos suit, and even then your survival can’t be guaranteed.

Which raises questions about the religious certainty so many possess. Why do we have a barrage of cocksure pronouncements about God coming at us from pulpits and books and TV evangelists and politicians and social crusaders? What about the doctrinal warfare, the spiritual empire building, the eagerness to condemn others to hell, the shoring up of denominational walls, and the fanaticism that throws bombs (symbolically or literally) at those who disagree? How can so many people be so sure about so many unseen things? Where is the humility that ought to temper religious conviction?

In the last book of the Bible, we read an odd phrase: "There was silence in heaven for about half an hour."[2] I heard a wag say that this will be to atone for all the sermons we've had to endure. Though the comment was in jest, I decided that if it's not true, it should be. Why only a half an hour, you ask? Wouldn't it take a few thousand years to deal adequately with all the world's sermons? Half an hour in heaven, keep in mind, is more than thirty minutes; it's part of eternity, so it would be half an hour unlike any other, half an hour without beginning or end, half an hour that's more than enough to answer the millions of sermons, some of which I myself have delivered.

I offer this not as an authoritative interpretation of the text but to make a point: all proclamations about God must be surrounded by silence—a silence that humbly kneels before the ineffable Mystery. When it comes to God, we're all blind and deaf and therefore ought to be, at least now and then, mute; we shouldn't hesitate to belly up to the bar of doubt and lift our glasses in praise of agnosticism. Who has a mind large enough and a spirit capacious enough to embrace deity?

Only God. Only God can understand God, and thus only God can speak trustworthily about God. *Therefore* knowledge of the divine must be knowledge we have received; it comes not from clever intellectualizing, imaginative speculation, or spiritual daydreaming but from quiet, attentive listening. We can know only what we are told.

Christian faith affirms that the One who is wholly other, who is obscured by the thick darkness of our ignorance, has shined a light of self-revelation. This divine Word, being personal, has a name: Jesus Christ.

{ .. .. }

This revelation, it should be noted, does two things: it shows God *and* it shows our ignorance. What Jesus Christ teaches about God leaves no doubt how wrong we've been. We could not have imagined *how much other* God really is. God is not only wholly other than humanity, but even wholly other than what we think God should be.

We might argue that we have some inkling of God, notwithstanding our limitations. The word *God,* after all, brings to mind *something;* it's not as if this chapter were about our chumminess with zitofloobergents, in which case we'd all be completely clueless. We share a general, rudimentary notion of deity, and what we know, surely, is that God is transcendent, exalted, strong, in control, the creator of life, and the enforcer of moral laws.

But if we sweep the table clean of preconceived expectations and pay attention to what we actually see in Jesus Christ, we're in for a surprise: our ideas about God are turned on their heads. Transcendent? What sort of transcendence clothes itself in human flesh? Exalted? What sort of exaltation manifests itself in abject humility? Strong? What sort of strength squirms and cries in a Bethlehem manger? In control? What sort of control surrenders to rejection, torture, and death? The creator of life? What sort of creativity ends up in the grave? The enforcer of moral laws? What sort of enforcement lavishes forgiveness on lawbreakers?

God may indeed be transcendent, exalted, strong, in control, the creator of life, and the enforcer of the moral code, but if this describes the God revealed in Jesus Christ, then each of these characteristics means more than we ever imagined; each somehow includes its opposite and must be seen upside down to be understood right side up. This is why I say that God is not simply other than us but also other than God, at least the way "God" is usually understood.

* * *

God doesn't stick to the job description; God apparently gets a kick out of playing hooky, breaking the rules, and shocking the universe out of its socks. God is unpredictable. *Exceedingly* unpredictable.

We would expect that a God who established the *laws* of nature and morality would be reliable. This expectation undergirds most religious practices. *If* we do such and such, *then* God can be counted on to respond appropriately: we pray, we participate in corporate worship, we do our best to obey the commandments, we give alms and perform good deeds—and we assume that if we do these things well, then

God will in some way reward us. Of course, we don't always get what we want; we still haven't won the lottery, and parking places don't always materialize; worse, our loved ones get sicker and sometimes they even die. Our disappointment might raise questions, possibly even doubt, but before long our assumptions snap back into place, and we get up another head of steam for our rituals. It's easier to think we haven't prayed fervently enough, say, than to accept the possibility that the God who hears our prayers may be different from what we imagine. We want (and think we need) a God who conforms to our expectations, which means a God who is, above all, useful: a God you can count on; a God who does what a God is supposed to do; a God who is, well, Godlike.

But the Word addressed to us in Jesus Christ forces us to acknowledge that God is far larger than our expectations. At first, this may not strike us as good news, for it leaves us with a distressingly unpredictable God.

Unpredictability, though, is in the eye of the beholder. What seems like unpredictability is, from God's standpoint, something else: absolute freedom. God is supremely free—free enough to be human, humble, and weak; free enough to lose control, enter death, and offer forgiveness; free enough to make binding promises, covenants, and commitments.

This freedom is the ground of grace. God can be gracious precisely because God cannot be contained by our understanding, cannot be restrained by sin, cannot be thwarted by death, cannot be limited by principles of justice, cannot even be kept within the boundaries of deity.

Chapter Four

For Us, Not Against Us

A COMPLETELY FREE God is more than a little unsettling, not the least because this means the end of religion.

Religion begins with a quest to understand God and then, once tenets become established, sets forth the appropriate human response. If your god resides in rocks, trees, and rivers, you worship the earth. If your god delights in the sacrifice of bulls, you build an altar and sharpen your knife. If your god promises paradise to martyrs of *jihad,* you strap on the bombs. If your god expects constant prayer, you grow calluses on your knees. If your god got the show rolling but is now AWOL, you do whatever you please. What you believe about God determines how you live.

The notion that religion is only a private concern, that in the end all spiritual beliefs are benign and should be affirmed, that what really matters is sincerity, that all we need to do is convene a parliament of religions and hold hands and sing "Kumbaya"—is, to put it as tactfully as possible, sheer stupidity. There are many images of God, and although they often share similarities they more often contradict, and even fiercely oppose, one another. Each of these images creates a belief system, which in turn establishes rituals and patterns of behavior—the cause, alas, of much of the world's conflict.

But what if God is absolutely free? What if God is unconstrained by human imagination and understanding? What if God can't be trusted to stay put in the religious boxes we've constructed?

We would have a serious problem. What's at stake is our ability to bargain with God, a fundamental motive of all religion. If God is such-and-such a being and if we behave appropriately, then we're more likely to find God's good side, more likely to receive goodies and avoid problems. So, for example, those of us who are Christians dedicate ourselves to obeying the Golden Rule, joining a congregation, worshiping enough to ensure that we're not just Christmas-and-Easter Christians, studying the Bible and praying, giving a portion of our income, and maybe even telling others about our faith. We often fail in our intentions, but we do our best to uphold our side of the bargain *in the hope* that God will uphold the other, really critical side of the bargain.

It's not difficult to cite vast stretches of the Bible that seem to support this arrangement. Didn't God enter into a *covenant*—a contract—with Israel and then with the Church? Didn't God issue the law, promising the blessings of obedience and threatening judgment against disobedience? Didn't God set forth the terms of the bargain?

Well, yes. But the parts of the Bible, even the lengthiest, must be read in the context of the whole; the entire story, from "In the beginning" to "Amen," tells us that God's covenant is first and foremost a covenant of grace, a consequence of God's prior decision to be *for* us. Gift came before obligation, and salvation before obedience. God created the universe; God shared the divine image, granting humans the capacity for love and relationship; God worked through Abraham and his descendents, starting history moving toward its redemption from rebellion; God delivered the Israelites from Egyptian slavery and only then gave the law to show grace-saved people how to live.

All this grace came to fullest expression in Jesus Christ. This is why not everyone was cheered by his presence; not everyone was happy about his miracles of healing and acts of compassion.

{ .. .. }

One Sabbath, early in his ministry, Jesus attended the synagogue. He was being a good Jew, but the religious leaders weren't about to give him any credit. They thought he was far too cavalier with the law, and they intended to keep an eye on him. You never knew what he might do, especially around someone in need. Not that there's anything wrong with compassion, mind you; mercy has its place. But you can't have people hacking down laws, like a logger cutting trees, or before long you will have destroyed the forest, and then what? What if Satan himself comes after you? What will protect you? You will have laid waste the chief expression of God's mercy. You can't let youthful concern for suffering—no doubt praiseworthy—carry you into reckless enthusiasm.

So on that day the religious leaders were also keeping an eye on someone else in the congregation, a fellow with a withered hand. A defect like that was just the sort of thing to light Jesus' fire. But the law commanded that no work be done on the Sabbath. None. Not even healing, the rabbis had decided. Now, Jesus could handle the situation appropriately if he had a mind to, if he had the necessary wisdom, if he really respected the law. He could say, "My friend, I see you've been suffering. I want to heal you. But first we must uphold God's purposes for all creation by respecting the commandments. So here's the deal: let's wait until six o'clock this evening, and I promise you, at one minute after six you'll have a new hand." An approach like this would demonstrate maturity, but would this young preacher have the spiritual chops for it?

Jesus knew what they were thinking, and according to Mark's account, "He looked around at them with anger; he was grieved at their hardness of heart." He was angry because they upheld the letter of the law at the expense of the spirit of the law. They worried more about breaking the law than fulfilling the law; they focused on abstract principles but lost sight of concrete people. They knew the laws but no longer knew the lawgiver; they remembered the edicts of God but forgot the heart of God. They could cite chapter and verse of the Bible, to be sure, but they had overlooked the whole point of the Bible and the chief purpose of the law: they had lost sight of grace.

"Stretch out your hand," Jesus said, and when the man did it, his hand was restored. The freedom of grace was enacted that day, and it was too much for the authorities. You can't have that much freedom running loose, especially in someone claiming to be God's representative.

You've got to nail it down, and the sooner the better.[1]

{ .. .. }

Why would the religious leaders of Jesus' day cling so tenaciously—so murderously—to the law, as though it were an end in itself? For the same reason we all do; for the same reason all religions have their rules and we work so hard to master them: to be able to bargain with God. The law imposes obligations on us, to be sure, but it might also lay obligations on God. If we obey it, we will earn a claim against God; we will become worthy to receive divine blessing.

Why do we really tend and protect a thick forest of laws? The answer may sound odd, even shocking: to protect us from God. It's the fundamental motive beneath all religious bargaining. Our modern chumminess with God turns out to be the nervous prattling of deep insecurity. We're actually afraid of God—and for good reason. We sense, sometimes consciously and always unconsciously, that things are not right between God and us. There's a problem and, although we can't exactly put a finger on it, it causes us a deep, rumbling disquiet. We're like Adam and Eve in the Garden of Eden, sensing the presence of God and hiding ourselves behind the trees. "Where are you?" God asks. Like Adam, we respond, "I heard the sound of you in the garden, and I was afraid, because I was naked; and I hid myself."

"Who told you that you were naked?" God asked Adam, and it was a good question, a question that stripped him bare, exposing far more than his body. What made Adam feel naked? What made him even come up with the concept of nakedness? For that matter, what made him say such a thing when he was actually clothed? Before they encountered God in the garden, Adam and Eve sewed fig leaves together for loincloths. Not haute couture, perhaps, but presumably adequate. So what made Adam feel so exposed, so vulnerable in the presence of the Creator?

Perhaps you're thinking, "They ate the apple." Actually, the text says nothing about apples. They could have eaten apples until their bowels groaned in misery; they could have munched them raw, baked pies, canned sauce, or fermented the best hard cider in the world—and God would have been more than pleased, probably even joined in the fun. The problem came with another fruit, which grew on the tree of the knowledge of good and evil. God had given them everything—the breath of life, the divine image, plants for food, one another for companionship—but God drew one boundary line, *just one,* and told them, "You shall not eat of the fruit of the tree that is in the middle of the garden, nor shall you touch it, or you shall die."

Of course, that was then the one fruit they wanted to try, the one they wanted most, the one they were sure would be the best in the garden. The serpent knew how to increase their desire and crush their dwindling resolve: "You will not die; for God knows that when you eat of it your eyes will be opened, and you will be like God, knowing good and evil."[2]

You will be like God. Here is the primal temptation, the most basic one known to humanity: to be like God. Grace had lavished the abundance of creation on our first parents, but it wasn't enough. It's never been enough, not for any of their descendents, including you and me. We want more: to be in God's place, which is to say, the center place; to be in control, if not of the whole universe, then of our universe.

{ .. .. }

If you find it difficult to swallow the account of creation in Genesis, it might help to remember the difference between literal facts and truth. Literal facts may be part of truth, but truth is always larger than and not dependent on literal facts. Jesus told parables—created fictions—and even though they don't refer to actual events they provide some of the clearest, most trustworthy teaching about God and us. In the same way, even if the stories at the beginning of Scripture are primeval parables, not literal history, they reveal truth to us, truth we immediately recognize because we see it played out all around us and most especially in us. We know how easy it is to believe a lie. We have plenty of experience coveting and grasping for things we know we can't have. We also want—desperately desire—to be at the center of our world, on top of things, in God's place. No one needs to convince us of the existence of Adam and Eve, because we've seen them dwelling in our own hearts!

There is a word that describes this falsehood, disobedience, and deadly pride: sin. You don't hear much about sin these days. After all, dwelling on it might damage our self-esteem, and that's something we're careful to guard against lest we end up in psychotherapy. But you know, speaking as someone who's been in psychotherapy, an interesting thing happens when we start digging into our lives, when we unflinchingly examine the choices we've made that have left the world a messier place, when we peel away the layers of probable influences that have shaped us for better or worse: we come at last to a dark core wrapped in a lie—a willful disobedience motivated by hungry arrogance. Sin, finally, is not so much a list of naughty things we sometimes do as a permanent affliction of self-centeredness.

After a couple of years of counseling, in which I tried to understand myself by excavating my past like an archeological dig, my psychotherapist looked up at me, sighed deeply, swept her arm through the air as though clearing the table of all the junk we had unearthed, and said, "Don, your problem is that you're a sinner. Isn't your religion supposed to deal with that?"

Judging from what I see around me, not mentioning any names, I'm not alone. Indeed, the Bible says that all have sinned. Every last one of us. Thus we all know, whether consciously or not, that things are not right, not the way they're supposed to be. In the deep recesses of our being, we feel at odds with God. We're afraid of being caught in our nakedness.

So we run for the trees. We need a tall, thick forest of laws we can hide behind. Give us the old-time religion—or for that matter, any religion at all that supplies plenty of laws. These laws threaten us, certainly, but they also offer the possibility that if we can get our act together, play by the rules, and score enough merit points, we just might escape with our lives. Religion gives us something to do; it gives us a place to hide.

We want to hide because we assume that God is mightily upset with us. By turning away from the source of life, we're faced with the opposite: death. That's not a happy prospect. So all our garrulous backslapping of the deity, our spiritual bonhomie, is like the exaggerated laughter of children convincing themselves they're not terrified of the dark. Underneath our fearlessness is really a profound fear: we expect that God will be against us.

But if we stay focused on Jesus Christ, the very one who at first threatens us with the revelation of an absolutely free God, if we stay with him as he takes upon himself our humanity, as he journeys to the cross, as he rises from the grave, we are led ineluctably to an overturning of our expectations: *God is not against us, but for us.* The freedom of God, as shown and defined in Jesus Christ, is not a willy-nilly freedom, but a freedom to be on our side, to be our advocate, to be the guarantor of our existence. The Apostle Paul asked, "If God is for us, who is against us? He who did not withhold his own Son, but gave him up for all of us, will he not with him also give us everything else? . . . I am convinced that neither death, nor life, nor angels, nor rulers, nor things present, nor things to come, nor powers, nor height, nor depth, nor anything else in all creation, will be able to separate us from the love of God in Christ Jesus our Lord."[3]

God is so much *for us,* the apostle concluded, that we may and must speak of God's *love* for us—a love, flowing from the heart of God, so secure and everlasting that nothing in all creation will be able to separate us from it.

In his autobiography, *Timebends,* Arthur Miller tells of his marriage to Marilyn Monroe. During the filming of *The Misfits* she descended into the depths of depression and despair. He feared for her life as he watched their increasing estrangement, her isolation from others, her paranoia, and her growing dependence on barbiturates. One evening, after a doctor had been persuaded to give her another shot and she was sleeping, Miller took the time to reflect in her presence. He said, "I found myself straining to imagine miracles. What if she were to wake and I were able to say, 'God loves you, darling,' and she were able to believe it! How I wish I still had my religion and she hers. It was suddenly quite simple—we had invented God to keep from dying of reality, yet love was the realist reality of all."[4]

Miller's longing in that moment was so tender it breaks your heart. But what if God were unconstrained by any religion? What if this freedom flashed forth most brilliantly in Jesus Christ? What if this revealed that the unfathomable and uncontrollable God was precisely this *for us?* Then we all could wake and hear, "God loves you, darling."

Chapter Five

Near, Not Distant

IMAGINE THAT YOU and I have been close friends, but for some reason you've wounded me. The wrong you've done could destroy our relationship, imprisoning us in its mischief; or it could be forgiven, freeing us for a new beginning. The latter can happen only if I'm able to rise above my resentment, above my wish to get even, and above my secret pleasure in being a victim. Rising this high will require Herculean freedom—freedom from myself and freedom for you—and there will be no forgiveness without it. Grace always requires freedom.

Project your imagination outward to the relationship between God and all creation, and you might catch a hint of the freedom necessary for God's grace. By that grace the universe was created, is sustained, and will be perfected. That much grace demands infinite freedom, the absolute liberty of a God who can rise high enough to stoop low, who can rise above transcendence to immanence, who can rise above omnipresence to limitation, who can rise above eternity to time.

God's ascent into grace, in other words, is a descent into human existence.

The prologue to the Gospel according to John says, "In the beginning was the Word, and the Word was with God, and the Word was God."[1] This Word, the personal self-revelation of God, "became flesh and lived among us, and we have beheld his glory, the glory as of a father's only Son, full of grace and truth."[2] These verses push language nearly to its breaking point; they compel us to speak of mysteries beyond our capacity of comprehension, things not illogical but beyond logic (not surprising, given the wild freedom of God): God, in a massive conspiracy of grace, has from all eternity willed to be both Father and Son, the Sender and the Sent, the One who, without ceasing to be God, becomes fully human. Later, as the story unfolds, we learn of the Holy Spirit, and we have to employ the ancient symbol of the Trinity; God, one in essence, is a triunity of persons—the perfect fellowship of Father, Son, and Holy Spirit. But for now, the important point is that the personal self-revelation of God, the Word, became flesh and, as the Greek indicates, moved into our neighborhood.

This incarnation—the enfleshment of God—was the first movement of the reconciliation between God and humanity, the first aspect of what we could call the Great Reversal. Whereas we have tried to rise to God's place, God has descended to ours; whereas we, in arrogance, have tried to seize control of our lives, God, in humility, has become weak and vulnerable; whereas we have tried to become larger and more important, God voluntarily became smaller and despised; whereas we have tried to storm heaven, God has claimed earth. If the essence of sin is pride, the first part of God's remedy is humility—a humility so decisive and absolute it could only flow from the heart of God.[3]

{ .. .. }

"That glorious form, that light unsufferable," John Milton wrote, "He laid aside, and, here with us to be, / Forsook the courts of everlasting day, / And chose with us a darksome house of mortal clay."[4]

God chose the "house of mortal clay" because that's where we live. The downward movement that reversed our pride was, at the same time, a pursuit in love, a following after the beloved into the depths of mortality.

My grandson Timothy is not quite two and a half years old. We talk a lot on the telephone because he lives about five hundred miles away. He jabbers on and on, and I understand only about half of what he says, if I'm lucky. Last evening, I told him his Grammy and I had bought him a present and sent it in the mail. He said, clear enough for me to catch it, "But would you bring it to me? I want you to come to my home."

He wanted us more than the present.

My eyes welled up as I tried to explain that we really wanted to come to his home, that we wanted to see him and hold him and play with him, but we couldn't because we lived a long way away. On the other end of the line, a sad little voice whispered, "A long way away."

Nothing can separate us from the love of God, Paul said, and that surely includes distance. But love always seeks to overcome distance; love wants to be near, not far. Love has within itself a restless energy that seeks to see and hold and share a life.

So God "chose with us a darksome house of mortal clay." That choosing, possible only because of God's unpredictable and uncontainable freedom to be *for* us, resulted in the most astonishing consequence, something we could not have predicted, given our notions about what God should be like. You'd have to be God to come up with it; you'd need a supremely free imagination. God chose to be un-Godlike, chose to put on flesh and become human, and the descent was both an act of humility that answered our pride and a pursuit of love that found us. In one movement, God cancelled our sin and embraced us, just as the father in Jesus' parable ran to meet his prodigal son, and in forgiving him embraced him and in embracing him forgave him. If the Christmas story doesn't knock us flat with wonder, we'd better check our pulse.

{ .. .. }

But this surprise can rather quickly turn into embarrassment. Thinking about the actual incarnation can transform the stoutly spiritual into the scrupulously squeamish. To be sure, hearing that God has come to our home appeals to our loneliness and warms our love-hungry hearts. But to discover just *how* near God has come can be discomforting.

I'm writing this chapter, it so happens, in early December. On one of our tables is a porcelain nativity set, with a cow, a donkey, three sheep, a shepherd, three wise men, an angel, and

Mary and Joseph—all gathered around the baby Jesus lying contentedly in a manger. Like much art of its kind, it has a detached, otherworldly quality about it. This is understandable, I suppose. We instinctively want to portray the advent of God's Son as beautifully as possible. Or perhaps, as sweetly as possible. The story is about the birth of a baby, after all, and when we see it reenacted in Christmas pageants, we especially enjoy the performances of children: Joseph in his dad's bathrobe, Mary holding her sister's dolly, the shepherds whacking each other with crooks. If our own kids are in it, we squat near the stage to record everything on video.

The real thing was neither beautiful nor sweet. To call it earthy would be closer to the facts. It was of this earth in which we live, where even our happiest moments often arrive mixed with fear, pain, and much messiness.

The birth took place in a backwater province of the Roman Empire, under questionable circumstances, with the "father" wondering exactly how his betrothed had become pregnant. It also happened at the most inconvenient time (as important events often do), when Joseph had to report to his hometown to register with the IRS. Everyone else was doing the same thing, and thus the roads were crowded and the inns filled.

Finding a place to stay became an urgent necessity when Mary's contractions started. But nothing was available in Bethlehem. The best Joseph could do was get permission to use a stable—a dank cave, most likely, filled with the tired, foaming animals of fellow travelers. There, on a pile dirty straw, Mary spread her legs and cried and whimpered and for a while didn't feel all that blessed, and Joseph stood around fretting and wondering what to do, and eventually the Son of God made his grand entrance into the world—bloody, wet, crying, and—not for the last time in his life—homeless.

The scene, as it happened, was nothing you'd want on a Christmas card. The baby, we can assume, was as cute as most newborns, which is to say adorable to his mother but too scrunched and splotchy to anyone else. Make no mistake about it, he did what all babies do: he fussed, got colic, and spit up; when Joseph changed his swaddling cloths for the first time, you can bet it wiped the smiles off shepherds' faces.

I don't mean to be crude. I simply want to stress an important point: in Jesus Christ the humiliation of God was complete. God came *all the way* into our human existence. God entered fully the time, the space, and the flesh we call home.

{ .. .. }

The usual human reaction to this story is to sanitize it. We remake the characters into porcelain art, cover them with gold leaf, and surround them with choirs of gorgeous angels singing Handel or Bach. We want to keep heaven in the forefront, keep the story *spiritual,* because the real thing was too coarse for good taste. Where's the inspiration in incessant crying, or sour spit-up, or infant feces?

The truth is, most of us have cleaved reality into two parts: the heavenly and the earthly. We're card-carrying dualists. We want God to be separate from our messiness, or else how can God save us from it? We want God to be clean, unsoiled by our humanity. A proper God, we think, could not *really* have become the flesh we know so well—not the tired, sweaty, belching, hungry, thirsty, farting, urinating, defecating, sniffling, coughing, sexual flesh that often embarrasses us and tempts us into all sorts of trouble. Any God worthy of the name would be above all this; any God worthy of adoration would only appear to have become incarnate.

To counter those who argued that the Son of God could not have appeared in an ordinary body, the epistle of I John begins by saying, "We declare to you what was from the beginning, what we have heard, what we have seen with our eyes, what we have looked at and touched with our hands, concerning the word of life . . ." and then goes on to explain that not every spirit is from God, but "every spirit that confesses that Jesus Christ has come in the flesh is from God."[5] Despite this affirmation, the heresy of Docetism (from the Greek *dokein,* to appear) has continued to thrive. Many still find it easier to believe that Jesus only *seemed* to be human.

A preference for dualism probably began in the Garden of Eden, when Adam was hiding behind the trees. If you feel naked and vulnerable, you hope God stays put and gives you space. A God who walks through the Garden (or puts on an infant's flesh) leaves no room to hide. A grace this aggressive raises questions. Couldn't the situation be handled with a lighter touch, a gentler approach? Couldn't God deal with human sin by simply letting bygones be bygones? Is it really necessary for God to come this deeply into human territory?

Is it really necessary for God to invade every square inch of our existence?

{ .. .. }

At first, this news about God is troubling, even frightening. If we stay with it, though, if we think our way more deeply into it—most of all, if we live in it—we discover a joy we could not have seen because of the disorientation caused by God's turning our world upside down in order to set it right side up. But once we adjust to the new reality, we hear something more in this news.

The birth of Jesus announces that God is near, not distant; it tells that God has claimed every part of our life, and thus when we say that God is *for* us we mean not only for our souls, not only for our spirituality, not only for our religious rituals, but for *all* of us. The divine descent is also the human ascent. By stooping to become one with us, God lifted our ordinary experience—its joys and sorrows, its pleasures and pains, its enthusiasms and routines—into new significance. God's purposes include *our* life and *our* world.

In case we miss this point in the Christmas story, the rest of the New Testament reaffirms it: Jesus used the most ordinary things to teach about God (lilies and birds, bread and wine); he died in the flesh and was raised with a transformed flesh (the Creed affirms the "resurrection of the body"); and he promised to come again (to this world). The embrace of God's grace includes the whole of human life.

The whole of our life. Dualism is no longer an option. We might still be tempted by it; we might, out of habit, continue to separate the heavenly from the earthly. But through the incarnation a marriage has taken place, and we dare not put asunder what God has joined together.

Why would we want to? This marriage liberates us from a conflicted existence. It assures us that our spirituality cannot be separated from our physicality; our relationship with God does not depend on denial of our humanity. The way to God, the incarnation tells us, is not to escape into a diaphanous realm, not to deny the flesh, not to suppress our ordinary drives and desires. Everything—the whole shebang!—has been invaded by God's presence and turned into an instrument of God's grace.

To be sure, asceticism has had an honored place in the practice of Christianity. But fasting, celibacy, or any other discipline of the body is a parenthesis within the grammar of ordinary life. No act of denial, however salutary, should be elevated to universal law. Ascetic practices show the relative worth of things, but because one thing is less valuable than another does not mean it should be despised. Fasting, for example, reminds us that eating is less important than prayer; nonetheless, there comes a time when you should get off your knees and put something in the oven. Although Jesus seemed to take it for granted that his followers would fast, he also commanded them to commune with him by eating bread and drinking wine.

"So, whether you eat or drink, or whatever you do," Paul said, "do everything for the glory of God."[6] It's not necessary to divide your life into sacred and secular spheres; it's not necessary to be torn between a spirit soaring into heaven and a body rooted to earth; it's not necessary to be more spiritual than God. Post-Christmas spirituality is *wholistic:* it refuses to tear apart the fabric of life but receives everything—eating pizza, praying, drinking pinot noir, listening to Bruce Springsteen, changing dirty diapers, fasting, listening to a friend, going to church, tickling a child, volunteering at hospice, visiting the zoo, reading the Bible, making love, laughing at a joke—as gifts to enjoy and offer back to God in gratitude.

Chapter Six

Revealed in Weakness, Not in Strength

THE BIRTH OF Jesus, according to Matthew's Gospel, fulfilled an ancient prophecy that declared, " 'Look, a virgin shall conceive and bear a son, and they shall name him Emmanuel,' which means 'God with us.' "[1]

Those three words perfectly summarize the meaning of Jesus—his life, death, and resurrection. He is God with us.

But before we take the lights off the tree and sweep up the straw from the pageant, questions elbow their way into our consciousness: If God is with us, why is there so much pain in this world? If God is near, not distant, why has each succeeding century been marred by bloody conflict? Why do millions of people—including innocent children—die every year from malaria, AIDS, and other diseases? Why is there so much racism and injustice? Why do bad things happen to good people, while good things happen to bad people? At a personal level, why is life so difficult—so laden with loneliness, fear, and sorrow?

If God is both for us and with us, why do we seem so much on our own?

There are no satisfying answers, at least none I've found. The problem of pain will trouble us as long as we stay attuned to our own hearts, not to mention what's going on around us. What we can do, though, is set it in a larger context, one that enables us to think differently about it and even find comfort in it. To do this, we must be attuned to God's heart, which means inquiring not about suffering in general but about Jesus' suffering in particular.

{ .. .. }

In what way is God with us? As we saw in the last chapter, God shares our humanity. Yes, *our* humanity: the humanity that has been broken by pride, disobedience, and falsehood; the humanity that is weak not simply because of finitude but because of failure; the humanity that, because it has turned its back on the source of life, now exists in the shadow of death.

All four Gospels begin the story of Jesus' ministry with John the Baptist. He was a desert-dwelling, bug-eating, fire-breathing preacher whose favorite way of addressing his congregation was to call them a bunch of snakes. He didn't fool around. God's Anointed One is bringing the Kingdom, he said, so you'd better not waste time cleaning up your life, turning to God, and getting baptized as a sign of your conversion. If you think I'm rough on you, he warned, just wait until the Anointed One arrives. He's going to bring God's righteousness down on you like a sharpened ax. It won't be a party.

But then Jesus showed up, and to John's surprise it *was* a party—one dinner party after another—and instead of whacking sinners, he embraced them. John told people to repent, and now John himself had to repent.

His change of heart began when, at the end of a sermon, he invited sinners to come forward for baptism. As the crowd hummed "Just as I Am," Jesus himself stepped toward the water. John protested, of course: "What do you think you're doing? You should baptize me!" But Jesus insisted, and together they waded into the Jordan River.

The *Son of God* submitting to a baptism of *repentance?* This is crazy—and a craziness that is precisely the place to begin if we want to understand what was happening. To repent, in the language of the Bible, is to turn one's mind and heart to God; it is to submit, wholly and unreservedly, to God's will. So why in the world would the embodiment of God need to turn toward God? Because he was in the world to redeem it. To cancel our arrogance, deity descended into flesh. God entered into the limitations of space, time, and bodily existence. God chose not simply finitude but the moral state of our finitude; God chose to stand shoulder to shoulder with those who need to clean up their lives, repent, and be baptized.

So Jesus surrendered himself to the arms of John, which pushed him under, burying him in water. Water, in the ancient Semitic world, was a dual-purpose symbol, indicating both life and death. The first is obvious, but the second is not and is perhaps best explained by a few images from the Old Testament. The earth was created when God separated the waters above the earth from the waters below the earth. All humanity was destroyed, save Noah and his family, in the waters of the flood. The children of Israel were delivered from Egyptian bondage when God divided the waters of the Red Sea. The Jewish exiles in Babylon were comforted by God's promise to be with them when they "passed through the waters," and they understood that this was an image of precreation chaos, of the terrors that threaten, of death itself. The baptism of Jesus, then, prefigured his whole life. He identified with humanity so completely that he plunged into the chaos resulting from turning away from the Creator; he plunged into the death that Adam and Eve and all their rebellious children justly deserve. What Jesus did in the Jordan was surrender himself not simply to John but to God, and some three years later the divine arms pushed him under and did not let him come up for air, burying him in death—a death unlike any other, a death that was, in effect, the fulfillment of death, a death that was absolute and eternal.

How could those arms let him drown? That's what Jesus wondered as he hung on the cross. His last words, according to Mark's Gospel, were, "My God, my God, why have you forsaken me?"[2]

This was the nadir of God's humiliation, the consummate response to our pride. We're forced to use contradictory language. Sin cleaved creation asunder, setting disobedient humanity against righteous God, and as God the Father abandoned God the Son the cleavage was taken into the being of God. Strange as it sounds, God became the godforsaken. God entered death, and death entered God.

{ .. .. }

Now, here is an astonishment worth pondering: this descent was at the same time an ascent. Jesus Christ, the Church contends, was fully God and fully human. Not half one and half the other, but wholly both. He was not only God with us but us with God; he was our representative, the one person who instead of disobeying did what God asked. Even as the Son of God went into the depths, the Son of Man rose to the heights; God at the nadir became humanity at the zenith.

To reverse the disobedience set in motion by our primeval ancestors—and pursued with creativity and enthusiasm by the rest of us—Jesus Christ was fully dedicated to God's will. His baptism was a sign of his entire life; he was *the* Repentant Human, the one who in every way was turned toward the Creator.

As the Apostle Paul argued, Jesus was the new Adam: "Therefore just as one man's trespass led to condemnation for all, so one man's act of righteousness leads to justification and life for all."[3] Adam's disobedience ruined creation, leaving his descendents broken and guilty and worthy of condemnation, but Jesus' obedience healed creation, leaving his brothers and sisters restored, forgiven, set free. In other words, as far as God is concerned, you and I are *in* Jesus Christ. His life is our life, his death is our death, and (as we'll see in the next chapter) his resurrection is our resurrection. As Jesus loved God and his neighbors, as he obeyed the commandments, as he spoke the truth and lived it in all his actions, as he befriended outcasts and healed the sick, as he forgave enemies who mocked and tortured him, as he laid down his life for his brothers and sisters, as he surrendered himself fully in obedience to God—as Jesus did what we wish we could do but can't because of our self-centeredness—*we did it in him.* We did everything God expects of us, and we did it perfectly!

{ .. .. }

The cross is the most well-known symbol of the Christian faith; we see it everywhere. It stands above church steeples, rests on altars, marks graves, hangs from ears, and bounces on breasts; it's made of wood, silver, gold, or covered with precious jewels. But know this: the event it bespeaks was a bloody, gruesome horror. Crucifixion at the hands of the Romans wasn't pretty. So how did the cross become a ubiquitous symbol of hope? Because of what it means: through Jesus Christ God "was pleased to reconcile to himself all things, whether on earth or in heaven, by making peace through the blood of his cross."[4]

To explain this reconciliation, the Bible uses various images and metaphors, drawn from Jewish tradition and the culture of the day—atonement, blood sacrifice, peace offering, ransom—as if no single one can convey all the meaning and mystery in it. If God was in Jesus Christ and if we are in him, no language, however sophisticated, and no image, however graphic, can adequately contain the truth of what happened that Friday outside the gates of Jerusalem on a hill called "the Skull." But the entire New Testament unanimously proclaims that a decisive transaction took place—a coming together of God and humanity that for all time and eternity destroyed the enmity, healed the wounds, forgave the sin, established peace, and saved a lost world.

Following Karl Barth, I have described the cross as the humiliation of God and the exaltation of humanity, the conclusive answer to our pride and disobedience. But the most important thing to remember is this: our rejection of Jesus, the defeat of the cross, was God's acceptance of us, the victory of grace. When human rebellion against God reached its most evil expression, God was most effectively at work for the restoration of creation.

{ .. .. }

This pushes us toward a startling, uncomfortable conclusion: if Jesus Christ is "the image of the invisible God,"[5] if we see in him the essential character of God, then we should expect that God's way into this world, God's trajectory into our lives, is to descend into our brokenness and death in order that we might ascend into healing and life. God is more often revealed in weakness than in strength.

This is not what we would expect. If the story were a Western, we would expect God to be the sheriff who courageously protects his town; we would not expect God to be the weakling who has to dance when the bullies shoot at his feet. If the story were a murder mystery, we would expect God to be the dashing detective who, through cleverness, solves the crime; we would not expect God to be the blood-soaked victim. If the story were a hospital drama, we would expect God to be the chief surgeon, in command of a cadre of nurses and technicians; we would not expect God to be the helpless patient.

As it is, the story we've been told confounds our expectations; God shows up as the weakling, the loser, the broken, the victim, the dying, the outcast. It's embarrassing, really. "We proclaim Christ crucified," Paul said, "a stumbling block to Jews and foolishness to Gentiles." How much salvation can come from a God who has been scorned, humiliated, beaten, and skewered to a cross to die? The world needs fixing, but won't it take a strong hand to do it, not one too weak to lift a finger?

Just as we're ready to get up from our pew to look elsewhere for help, Paul transitions to his next point, and what we hear is so absurd it might well be true, so unexpected it might well have come from another realm: "For God's foolishness is wiser than human wisdom, and God's weakness is stronger than human strength. . . . God chose what is foolish in the world to shame the wise; God chose what is weak in the world to shame the strong; God chose what is low and despised in the world, things that are not, to reduce to nothing things that are, so that no one might boast in the presence of God."[6]

What we have in the humiliation of the Son of God and the exaltation of the Son of Man, what we have in this revolting spectacle of the cross, is nothing other than the unrelenting pursuit of grace—a grace so prodigal and reckless in its intent that it goes to the most unlikely of places. Grace gravitates, with gathering force, to where it's most needed. So we must understand this: we are more likely to meet God not on the mountaintop of insight but in the valley of doubt, not in proud accomplishment but in humiliating failure, not in moral victory but in immoral defeat, not in wholeness but in brokenness, not in strength of spirit but in poverty of spirit. "Blessed are the poor in spirit," Jesus said, "for theirs is the kingdom of heaven."[7]

{ .. .. }

After World War I, the Prince of Wales visited injured soldiers in a military hospital. He went from bed to bed thanking the men for their sacrifices for Great Britain. As he left the ward, he said to the official in charge, "You told me there were thirty-six soldiers here, but I counted only twenty-nine. Where are the other seven?"

The official replied that the others were wounded so severely they would likely never leave the hospital. "It would be better to leave them alone."

Undaunted, the Prince entered that ward and spoke to each soldier as he did in the first. But as he left, he noticed there were only six. "Where is the missing soldier?" he asked.

"Ah, Your Majesty, he is in a dark room by himself. He is blind, mute, deaf, and completely paralyzed by the injuries he suffered. He awaits release by death."

The Prince of Wales quietly opened the door to the room and saw the poor creature lying upon his bed. It was impossible to express sympathy or gratitude, or even to shake the man's hand. So the Prince went over to the bed, stooped over him, and kissed him on the forehead.[8]

In the dark room of our existence, wounded by life and waiting for death, we feel a kiss on our forehead. A great compassion stoops over us and enfolds us.

{ .. .. }

What, then, of human suffering? We still have no answers, and we are left with our pain and the feeling that we've been abandoned by God. But as we cry, "My God, my God, why have you forsaken me?" we suddenly realize that despite our urgency and despair, our lament is a faint echo of something we've heard before, and we remember the words of our god-forsaken Brother.

We know we're not alone.

Instead of answers, we have been given a Presence.

Chapter Seven

Rule Breaker, Not Rule Maker

FOR MANY PEOPLE, God is the Great Umpire in the Sky who got the game going, set down the rules, and is more than ready to send violators to the Penalty Box, if not to the shower. Which, if true, means we're in big trouble. A recent cartoon in the *New Yorker* shows an angel speaking to a new arrival at the pearly gates, and the caption says, "Actually, he's not all that big, but he's really ripped."[1]

But by now it should be clear that the caption should read, "Actually, he's bigger than you think, but he's not impressed with rules." God refuses to act like a proper god, as we have seen, and with surprising freedom has chosen to be for us—*for us* to the extreme, to the point of bearing both the burden of our flesh and the responsibility for our sin. The birth of Jesus in a Bethlehem stable and his crucifixion on a cross have revealed grace that is more than amazing, grace that has gone far beyond the rules.

To be sure, rules have their place. When human beings decided to turn away from God and head down a road that would end in death, God imposed rules—the law—as a kind of temporary expedient, as a way to hold things together until the fullness of eternal love could be revealed. But this came *after* God renewed the covenant with creation and blessed Noah and his descendents; and *after* God chose Abraham and his family, promising to be their God and to give them a land of their own; and *after* God delivered some of that family, the Israelites, from Egyptian slavery—*after* grace had done its work. The law, it should be noted, was actually a part of this grace; its purpose was to show people how best to live and be together in community. "Do not covet," it said, and "do not murder" and "do not commit adultery" and so on, not because God wanted to throw a wet blanket on our fun but as a warning, as in "do not jump off the roof of a tall building." The law was the Creator's manual on how best to survive and thrive.

But given the human inclination toward pride, disobedience, and falsehood, given our radical self-centeredness tearing apart creation, the law could never be the ultimate solution. We would always use it as trees in the garden, as a way of hiding from God; we would use it for protection, for making claims against God. If we kept the rules, God would be obliged to bless us and stay out of our way. So the law, however well it might restrain the worst of human mischief, would always come between us and God, not unlike the way a contract stands between individuals by acknowledging their basic untrustworthiness.

But what if the Creator fashioned us for fellowship? What if God wanted to love and to be loved and thus to establish intimate communion with us? Well, think about it this way: what if you and your spouse only related to one another through agreed-on rules? What if you only celebrated your marriage on the anniversary of your wedding, and only honored one another on birthdays, and only said "I love you" at 7:00 A.M. every day, and only had sex every other Saturday evening? You might be scrupulous with these rules, never breaking them, but eventually they wouldn't mean much. A loving relationship can't be sustained by law.

God's rules, as helpful (in their way) as they are, had to be transcended. Grace gave the law, but inevitably grace had to burst through its own gift, had to be set free from its limitations. So along came Jesus, and the Gospels make clear that one reason he was nailed to a cross was because he challenged the system: he was too free, too cavalier about the law, too much a rule breaker. He embodied a love that was far larger than could be contained in any rule.

The system—a world of cause and effect, law and its consequences—came down on Jesus with full force; its ultimate sanction was always death. Break the law, you're punished; break the law in a big way, you're dead. So Jesus was put to death with the exquisite efficiency of Roman crucifixion; he was made as dead as dead gets, in other words, as indisputably and irrevocably dead as possible; he was buried in a tomb, a big rock was rolled in front of it, and a seal was set. It was all over for Jesus. Finished. The rules were dancing in triumph on top of the grave.

{ .. .. }

But something wholly unexpected happened: God raised Jesus from death. This is the witness of the earliest disciples, the unanimous testimony of the New Testament writers, and the conviction that gave birth to the Christian movement. The Gospels tell the story in slightly different ways, but they agree that three days after his burial Jesus was no longer in his tomb, and that he appeared to his followers. This transformed his followers from being dispersed, dispirited, and doubt-filled to being connected, courageous, and confident; it turned them inside out and made them turn the world upside down.

Or rather, the Resurrected One commissioned them to be witnesses of God's turning the world upside down. The resurrection of Jesus meant that death itself had been buried, and thus all other certainties had been nullified, save one: the grace of God. This was news worth proclaiming.

Since Adam's and Eve's departure from the Garden, humanity had lived with the certainty of death. You live, you die. This was the unassailable fact, the proof of a predictable world—a world that, in the physical sphere, operates by cause and effect and, in the moral sphere, by law and consequences. If *this,* then *that.* But when Jesus emerged from the tomb, it was as though God, in rebellion against the reign of rules, broke the power by which every rule works. Rules depend on sanctions, and the mother of all sanctions is death. By destroying the ultimate threat, God undermined the existing order and overturned everything. The only certainty remaining was the freedom of God—a freedom that, through the birth and death of Jesus, had shown itself to be a freedom *for us,* a freedom that is nothing other than the resolve of grace.

{ .. .. }

To understand what energized those earliest witnesses, we must recall a central point of the last chapter: Jesus was the Son of Man, the Representative Human. He was one of us, and by God's gracious and wildly free fiat, we are in him. This means that even as his death was our death, so also his resurrection is our resurrection, the promise that for us too life will be triumphant. This is what Paul wanted the believers in Corinth to grasp: "Christ has been raised from the dead, the first fruits of those who have died. For since death came through a human being, the resurrection of the dead has also come through a human being; for as all die in Adam, so all will be made alive in Christ."[2]

The glory of Easter is not simply that one corpse was resuscitated in a far corner of the Roman Empire, but that in this corpse, *in Christ,* the resurrection of humanity has started. Death has been defeated, for us and for everyone else. True, this is not always evident. As I write this chapter, newscasters are reporting an earthquake in Iran that killed more than thirty thousand people, another attack on U.S. soldiers in Iraq, a mudslide in southern California that killed fourteen people in a church camp, and an avalanche in Utah that killed two snowboarders; we all have friends and family who have passed away or who are perhaps near death. If Paul could rhetorically ask, "Where, O death, is your victory?

Where, O death, is your sting?" we could truthfully respond, "Since you asked, just about everywhere you look." We seem to be standing on the edge of a vast grave; the dirt beneath our feet is crumbling, and we are falling into the hole of our mortality. Death's victory, however, is only apparent; death's sting will not endure. We still live on the Good Friday side of Easter; we could say that we are living through a very long Saturday. But the raising of Jesus—if he was truly our Representative, the one who bears our destiny—means that Sunday is coming.

Jesus' resurrection will be our resurrection, and the New Testament wants us to understand this in two ways. It will happen in the future when we are lifted out of our own graves. This is the far horizon of our hope; this will be the consummation of Christ's victory. "Each in his own order: Christ the first fruits, then at his coming those who belong to Christ. Then comes the end."[3] But resurrection is also a present experience; it happens today. Even as we suffer minideaths—depression, illness, failed relationships, and the countless losses we endure—before we're finally laid to rest, we also experience miniresurrections—joy, healing, forgiveness, new beginnings—before the angelic trumpeter blows the final reveille. "I came," Jesus said, "that they may have life and have it abundantly."[4]

{ .. .. }

Frederick Buechner wrote, "He rose. A few saw him briefly and talked to him. If it is true, there is nothing left to say. If it is not true, there is nothing left to say. For believers and unbelievers both, life has never been the same again."[5] What Buechner means, of course, is that if it is not true, the story is over, once and for all, and there is no reason to mention it again. If Jesus was not resurrected, his birth is not worth remembering, his teaching has no authority, and his crucifixion bears no significance, except to leave no doubt that in the end death always wins. But if it is true, if Jesus was resurrected, then there is still nothing left to say, in the sense that we are left speechless, not simply from amazement but because the final truth about Jesus and us has been spoken. The resurrection confirms that, yes, God was indeed in that baby squealing and squirming in a Bethlehem manger; and yes, God was indeed speaking through the itinerant preacher from Nazareth; and yes, God was present in the godforsaken death of the cross; and yes, God was indeed in all of this because God is bent on restoring a broken creation and saving a lost world.

The resurrection of Jesus is a spotlight beaming from the empty tomb. It illuminates what God has been up to all along, from the beginning of time: it shows that God's heart beats with the rhythm of grace, and its insistent pulse will draw all creation into a dance of love. For this to happen, sin's damaging consequences had to be reversed, and that took drastic measures. Our pride had to be canceled by a more powerful humility; our disobedience had to be annulled by a more powerful obedience; and our falsehood had to be dispelled by a more powerful truth. The light of the resurrection, then, is the final response to our sin, the Truth that conquers the lie that began when the tempter suggested our first parents could actually become like God, and the lie that continues into the present whenever we arrogantly try to seize heaven's throne or slothfully refuse to become the men and women we were created to be. This light reveals who we really are: creatures wholly dependent on the grace of God. And this light reveals who God really is: the Creator who intends to remake creation.

Remake creation. The resurrection of Jesus tells us that God desires nothing less than to remake us. God is not interested, apparently, in letting bygones be bygones; God wants to do more than put a spiritual shine on our lives; God intends something far more radical than to renew us, or help us release our latent potential, or assist us along the way of our spiritual journey. What God plans for us can never be explained by analogies from our experience; lilies blossoming, butterflies emerging, or chicks hatching just don't convey it, despite the desperate attempts of too many Easter sermons. Resurrection is the *completely* new thing, and that's what God intends for us: to resurrect us, to remake us *ex nihilo,* to create something new out of nothing.

If we need resurrection, then, we have to conclude the obvious: we're dead. The death that entered the world because of sin has already reached its icy tentacles into our lives. A few years ago a movie was made about a prisoner on death row; it was called *Dead Man Walking.* That's what we all are, if resurrection is what we need. We may be walking, carrying on with things as best we can, perhaps in the illusion that everything is going well for us, but from God's standpoint we're dead. Sin—our own and that of others—

has had more deleterious consequences than we realize; we're as good as dead.

What do dead people do to help themselves? Nothing. Nada. Zip. Zilch. Zero. The dead don't embark on a program of self-improvement or of renewal—both of which depend on at least a spark of life. The dead are not on any sort of a spiritual journey. The dead do nothing, not a thing. They *cannot* help themselves. They are wholly and irrevocably dependent.

On what? On a God who specializes in bringing something out of nothing, who seems to love nothing so much as blowing warm breath into cold lips. The dead are saved, in other words, not by works but by grace. This is exactly what was promised in the resurrection of Jesus.

The Truth shining from an abandoned tomb reveals both the seriousness of our plight and the sufficiency of God's cure. We have no hope other than this cure, and this cure—grace—is more drastic than we could have imagined.

Chapter Eight

Passionate, Not Unmoved

All right, let's acknowledge a question getting more insistent with each chapter of this book: What about God's judgment? You don't need a doctorate in theology to know that many parts of the Bible show a God who can be, well, really ripped. Adam and Eve get thrown out of the Garden, the world is flooded by a deluge, the Israelites have to spend forty years in the wilderness, assorted kings end up on the wrong end of the sword, prophets announce impending doom, and sure enough the doom arrives when Assyria hauls off Israel and Babylonia levels Judah. By the time you come to the end of the Old Testament, you have the strong impression that you'd better not cross God, if you know what's good for you. The New Testament, too, has dire warnings of fearsome judgment, climaxing in scenes from Revelation that can turn your legs to jelly and keep you awake at night.

If God is love, how do we explain the many passages of Scripture that speak of God's wrath against sin?

Now is precisely the time to ask this question, after we have focused on the birth, death, and resurrection of Jesus Christ. God was busily engaged in human history for many centuries, of course—liberating Israel, providing a promised land, raising up kings, sending prophets—but God's most complete self-disclosure came in Jesus Christ. "Long ago God spoke to our ancestors in various ways by the prophets," begins the Letter to the Hebrews, "but in these last days he has spoken to us by a Son, whom he appointed the heir of all things, through whom he also created the worlds. He is the reflection of God's glory and the exact imprint of God's very being."[1] Or as Paul put it, in Christ "the whole fullness of deity dwells bodily."[2] We best understand God's character, then, by starting here, at the center, and working outward; we best see God's purposes as the light of the empty tomb illuminates the entire sweep of history.

If Jesus Christ is the one through whom the worlds were created, we must assume that God is consistent, not fickle, not constantly shifting from Plan A to Plan B and then on to Plan C. God didn't undergo a personality change between the Old and New Testaments, metamorphosing from a wrathful Judge into a loving Father sometime between Malachi and Matthew. No, Jesus Christ was no afterthought, but the one in whom we have been chosen "before the foundation of the world."[3] The grace we see in him, in other words, has been God's motivation from before time; from eternity, God has willed to embrace creation in love.

"God is love."[4] It's worth noting that this biblical declaration does not tell us that God is love and wrath, or love and judgment, or love and anything else. Love shares its billing with no other attribute because love alone describes God's *essential* character. This means that if we see evidence of divine judgment against sin—and surely we do—this judgment must be a consequence of love in relationship with a rebellious world. God's wrath is not an end in itself but an unlikely instrument of grace.

{ .. .. }

Love wants the best for the beloved.

A few days ago, I was speaking with my daughter on the telephone. In the background I could hear the sounds of Timothy, her two-and-a-half-year-old son, and Daniel, his baby brother; Timothy was singing, as best I could tell, and Daniel was crying.

Suddenly Jennifer hollered, "No, Timothy! You may not hit Daniel in the head with Noah's ark! You stop that right now!" Then she said to me, "Uh, sorry, Dad, but I've got a crowd control issue here."

I fully understood because, after all, Jennifer had once been a two-and-a-half-year-old too, and though I don't remember that she ever hit her sister with Noah's ark she did other things that required disapproval, and on rare occasions deserved punishment. When I disciplined her, was it because I simply lost patience? To be honest, there might have been a bit of frail humanity in my reactions, but the largest part of my motivation was always love—a love that wanted her to learn that there were boundaries in life, wanted her to learn how to behave in the presence of others, wanted the best for her. It is difficult to discipline well and wisely, but every good parent does it. We give a toddler a "time out"; we forbid a child to watch a favorite TV program; we ground a preadolescent for two weeks; we push an adolescent into a drug program. Love that will not, when appropriate, make demands and enforce sanctions is a flabby counterfeit. Authentic love has a stern side.

In Dostoyevsky's *The Brothers Karamazov,* Father Zossima says, "Love in action is a harsh and dreadful thing, compared with love in dreams."[5]

Why would it be different with God's love? God is for us, and thus God must necessarily be against all that harms or hinders us. When we ourselves are doing the harming or hindering, we expose ourselves to the possibility of divine punishment—a punishment, though, that aims not at retribution but at reformation. Sometimes, according to Scripture, God simply allows the consequences of sin to overwhelm us. "For a brief moment I abandoned you," God said to the exiles in Babylon who had foolishly ignored the prophets' warnings, "but with great compassion I will gather you. In overwhelming wrath for a moment I hid my face from you, but with everlasting love I will have compassion on you, says the Lord, your Redeemer."[6] Sometimes, we're told, God punishes us directly. The writer of the New Testament Letter to the Hebrews wanted his readers to buck up, to endure the difficulties they were undergoing, so he reminded them of a familiar proverb: " 'My child, do not regard lightly the discipline of the Lord, or lose heart when you are punished by him; for the Lord disciplines those whom he loves, and chastises every child whom he accepts.' . . . God is treating you as children; for what child is there whom a parent does not discipline? . . . Now, discipline always seems painful rather than pleasant at the time, but later it yields the peaceful fruit of righteousness to those who have been trained by it."[7]

{ .. .. }

Judgment happens because God cares. The God of the prophets, the Father of Jesus Christ, is not an abstract idea, not an unmoved mover, not an aloof deity. The God we encounter in the Bible is not only infinite but intimate; God is personally involved and concerned about us. The Jewish rabbi Abraham Heschel says the secret to understanding Jeremiah, Isaiah, and the other prophets was that they had an overwhelming experience of God's pathos, which "denotes not an idea of goodness, but a living care; not an immutable example, but an outgoing challenge, a dynamic relation between God and man . . . no mere contemplative survey of the world, but a passionate summons."[8]

But Rabbi Heschel doesn't characterize God as passionate, because the latter, he says, refers to "drunkenness of the mind, an agitation of the soul devoid of reasoned purpose, operating blindly."[9] He's the cautious scholar here—in my judgment too cautious, making distinctions that wouldn't have occurred to the prophets as they were swept along in the river of God's concern for humanity. Human passion, to be sure, is sometimes devoid of purpose, but not always. A man may have perfectly sound reasons for loving a woman, having chosen a partner whose strengths complements his weaknesses, and yet still be giddy with affection. If human passion can coexist with wisdom, surely God's can also—and with perfect balance.

From our standpoint, however, God's passion might well appear unreasonable. Brennan Manning refers to a scene from *Gideon,* a play written by a Brooklyn Jew named Paddy Chayefsky:

> Gideon is out in the desert in his tent a thousand miles from nowhere, feeling deserted and rejected by God. One night, God breaks into the tent and Gideon is seduced, ravished, overcome, burnt by the wild fire of God's love. He's up all night, pacing back and forth in his tent. Finally dawn comes, and Gideon in his Brooklyn Jewish accent cries out, "God, Oh God, all night long I've thought of nuttin' but You, nuttin' but You. I'm caught up in the raptures of love. God, I want to take You into my tent, wrap You up, and keep You all to myself. God, hey, God tell me that You love me." God answers "I love you, Gideon."
>
> "Yeh, tell me again, God."
>
> "I love you, Gideon."
>
> Gideon scratches his head. "I don't understand. Why? Why do You love?"
>
> And God scratches His head and answers, "I really don't know. Sometimes, My Gideon, passion is unreasonable."[10]

God *is* passionate. We shouldn't hesitate to use this word because it best describes the nature of God's involvement with this world. It comes from the Latin *passio* and the Greek *pascho,* which mean suffering. To be passionate is to care so deeply it hurts, to be so intimately involved it causes suffering.

Eugene Ormandy once so passionately directed the Philadelphia Philharmonic that he threw his arm out of joint. He gave himself so completely to the music it maimed him. That's not a bad way to picture God: directing the music so intensely it causes suffering. God cares how each of us plays our part, cares deeply enough to throw the baton at us when we fall asleep, cares deeply enough—I can't help it, I feel myself giving way to a parade of metaphors—to become a hurricane that blows down everything shoddily built, cares deeply enough to become a hammer that pounds all opposition into submission, cares deeply enough to become a raging river that relentlessly sweeps away all debris, cares deeply enough to become a fire that consumes all dross in the white heat of love.

In God's presence, indifference gets slapped to alert attention, pretension gets knocked on its backside, and disobedience gets its just reward. Given our familiarity with these things, we have to conclude that God is definitely not safe. If we recall that God is also wildly unpredictable, our knees will really start knocking in fear.

But just as we're ready to run for cover, we remember that God's dangerous freedom did something so wholly unnecessary, so completely unexpected, so beyond human rationality that it seems, yes, a drunkenness of the mind, an insane passion: God maintained both the demands of justice and the needs of mercy by entering our flesh and bearing the responsibility for our sin. Then, just as it would appear that the Law had indeed won, that it had proven its superiority even over eternal love, Jesus was raised from the grave, which crushed forever the death-dealing rules and put death itself in the grave.

The passion of God led to the passion of Jesus Christ. God's wrath against sin and God's mercy toward us become one and the same in Jesus Christ, a single movement of salvation. On the cross, the sin of humanity (mine, yours, and everyone else's) was damned to hell, given exactly what it deserved and chose for itself: separation from God. But because this happened in the Son of Man, our Representative, and because he was also the Son of God, the Beloved, we witness an astonishing turn of events: the Judge took the place of the judged.

But this was no victory for abstract justice, for the passion of God burst through legalism, burst through the necessity of judgment, burst through earthly authority—political and religious—and burst *into* the life-dealing freedom of grace. Easter proved that the passion of God would respect no limits but do everything necessary to secure the best for the beloved—including the re-creation of resurrection.

Like Paddy Chayefsky's Gideon, we say, "Why?"

And with a laughter both unfamiliar and long known, we hear this: "Sometimes, my dear, passion is unreasonable."

Chapter Nine

Therefore Risk Trust

THE GOD REVEALED in Jesus Christ is an upside-down deity. How better can we describe a God who is unpredictably free and demonstrates this freedom by refusing to play by the rules and stay in heaven, instead taking a passionate dive of downward mobility to be with us—with us in our flesh, with us in our brokenness, with us in our death-bound humanity? This Emmanuel ("God is with us") is the personal embodiment of an act of humility that reverses our pride and an act of obedience that reverses our disobedience—and we know this because of Easter, which proclaims *the* truth, about God and us, and thus reverses our falsehood. The resurrection tells us that God is not a deity to be feared, but a God who breaks the rules in order to remake us and embrace us with a love that will not let us go.

To put it as succinctly as possible, *God is for us.* The whole sweep of Scripture, when read from its interpretative center outward, proclaims a single message: the triumph of God's grace in Jesus Christ. God has determined to be on our side, to be our advocate, to heal us from our wounds, and to guarantee us not simply a second chance but also a third and fourth and fifth—chances without end. God has made an irrevocable decision to embrace us with a love that will never—come hell or high water, come external opposition or internal weakness, come legions of angry demons or the Pale Rider himself—never, never, *never* let us go. In the words of the Letter to the Ephesians:

> God, who is rich in mercy, out of the great love with which he loved us even when we were dead through our trespasses, made us alive together with Christ—by grace you have been saved—and raised us up with him and seated us with him in the heavenly places in Christ Jesus, so that in the ages to come he might show the immeasurable riches of his grace in kindness toward us in Christ Jesus. For by grace you have been saved through faith, and this is not your own doing; it is the gift of God—not the result of works, so that no one may boast.[1]

{ .. .. }

We are now in "the ages to come," and thus our present delight and duty is to learn of God's immeasurable grace and immerse ourselves in it. If from time to time we must ask what it means that we have been saved by grace "through faith," if we must inquire about our response to God's initiative, this should only come *after*—after we have been startled out of ourselves by the greatness of grace. The objective must come before the subjective;

what God has done for us, outside us, and despite us must come before we give even a second's consideration to our personal response.

Unfortunately, the subjective always tries to overwhelm the objective, and it's usually successful. Because our feelings are so immediate, so inescapable, we're easily and willingly seduced away from the fact of God's love into the quicksand of subjectivity. Do I have enough faith or too much doubt? Am I praying properly? Should I be mastering different spiritual techniques? Why don't I sense God's presence?

We're not helped much by well-meaning preachers and authors who apparently find it easier or more interesting to crack the whip of the imperative ("Do this!") than announce the news of the indicative ("God has done this!"). Go to the religious section of your local bookstore and peruse the titles. What do you see? Books that promise to increase your faith, or heal you, or teach you to pray, or shape you up in one way or another. We buy these books, too, because they're "practical"; we want tools to tune up our own souls and help us be better people.

But the problem is this: spiritual self-absorption is still self-absorption. Remember, the essential structure of sin is self-centeredness; what we need most is not to baptize this structure but to be delivered from it. This is why I'm uncomfortable that some churches invite people to "accept Jesus" or to "invite Jesus into your life." As long as *I* invite Jesus into *my* life, I'm able to keep me at the center. Jesus may be an important part of my life, adding a wonderful new dimension, but I'm still in control. Grace wants something far more radical: it wants to save me from myself, to convert me, to turn me toward God.

How does this happen? The good news of God's grace in Jesus Christ has the power to throw us off-center, to destabilize us. This is because the Word of creation ("all things came into being through him") and the Word of redemption ("the Word became flesh and lived among us")—the living Jesus Christ—continues to work through the announcement of the Gospel. If we stop our navel gazing and pay attention, we will hear that God has loved us from before the foundation of the world and will continue to love us for all eternity, and that this God has already lifted us into a cleansing and life-renewing embrace. This can be a loving slap on the cheek, just what we need to bring us out of hysterical self-absorption.

But alas, the pull of self-absorption is so great that no sooner do we come around to reality than we slide again into subjectivity: we take the pulse of our faith, we measure the cholesterol of our doubt, we check the blood pressure of our spiritual fervor, and we might even start a training program to increase our strength. But nothing will make us sicker than this preoccupation with health. The most important thing we can do to help ourselves is to forget ourselves.

{ .. .. }

With much caution, I bring up the matter of faith. It's a dangerous subject, given our temptation to stay focused on anything that has to do with us, but it can't be avoided. "For by grace you have been saved through faith," we're told, and thus we must ask what this means.

Although the Bible speaks about faith, it's really not much interested in faith *per se.* The power of faith may be a theme that fascinates preachers, televangelists, and authors, but it holds no interest for the writers of Scripture. Their concern is the power of God, and if they mention faith it's only to show the appropriate response to what God has already done or promised. The Bible, for example, knows nothing of faith healing; rather, it tells about *God's* healing and what that can do for individuals. Faith is a reaction, and the reaction is never half as important as what triggered it. When the Bible does discuss faith, it shows how faith works, what it does. True, the writer of Hebrews hazards an abstract definition ("Now faith is the assurance of things hoped for, the conviction of things not seen"), but as if he knows it's not much help spends the next thirty-nine verses giving example after example of people who lived faithfully.[2]

The great example of faith is Abraham, one of the first characters we meet in Scripture. For some reason, God decided to get the history of salvation rolling through him; to kick things off God promised him a new homeland and plenty of posterity. That got Abraham's attention, especially since he and the missus were childless and getting along in years. So what did Abraham do? Well, after what had to be an interesting conversation with Sarah ("What do you mean, he spoke to you? Who's *he?*"), he packed up his household and headed west, and I imagine that as often as he could get away with it he doused himself with cologne and spread rose petals on their bed. He acted, that's the point. He knew nothing about the God who had addressed him, and I would guess that he had plenty of doubts about whether it really was God he had heard or his own imagination, but at some point he decided to trust that the promise was real. Had you asked him about his faith, he wouldn't have known what you were talking about. Faith? There was nothing particularly "spiritual" in what he did. He had heard a promise, and in his own self-interest he acted on it.

This is faith at its most basic. In the New Testament, "faith" and "belief" come from the same Greek word: *pistis.* Occasionally this refers to the tradition—beliefs and practices—of the church ("contend for the faith that was once for all entrusted to the saints"[3]), and occasionally it indicates intellectual consent ("even the demons believe—and shudder"[4]), but most often it means trust. To have faith, in the biblical sense, is to entrust oneself to God. Abraham heard a promise and decided to believe it. God told him to go west, so he packed up the camels; God said he would be the father of multitudes, so he fired up his love life. He did what he was told because he trusted the One who spoke to him. Faith describes a particular relationship.

{ .. .. }

In Jesus Christ, God has promised that we've already been saved by grace, that the heavy lifting of redemption has been done, that all of us prodigal sons and daughters are home free because of a father who's raced down the road to throw his arms around us. It's as if God has said, "Look! See that baby in a manger wearing your flesh? See that broken body on a cross bearing your sins? See that risen Lord promising you victory over death—see how much I love you? Now, won't you finally trust me?"

Why wouldn't we trust such a God? What reasonable choice do we have?

Imagine yourself swimming in the middle of a lake. For some reason, because of cramps or weariness, you know you can't get back to the shore, and there's no boat in sight. You holler and wave your arms, but to no avail. Going down for the third time, you're beginning to see the instant replay of your life as the water fills your lungs. Just then a strong arm grabs you and pulls you to the surface. A voice says, "Relax, I've got you, trust me." Would you say, "No, I want to do it on my own, thank you very much"? Or would you say, "No, I prefer to be rescued by someone else"? I dare-say that without a moment's hesitation you would become a convert: you would have faith in your savior, and you would be saved through this faith, only to the extent that it enabled you to receive, without obstruction, the gift of salvation.

Of course, some choose not to have faith in God, preferring to take their chances with themselves or to hope in other people. But if Jesus Christ really reveals the heart of God, we have to wonder why. Such unbelief, Karl Barth rightly noted, is an "impossible possibility." It is a possibility, apparently, because some people do it; but given the fearful consequences and the sheer stupidity of it, it can only be considered an *impossible* possibility.

Perhaps you are thinking, "Wait a minute! If I were drowning in the middle of the lake and someone grabbed hold of me, I would feel his wet skin and hear his voice and maybe smell lake water in his hair. But when it comes to God—well, that's different. I don't see anything, don't hear anything, and I'm not even 100 percent sure God exists. So how can I trust, with this doubt?"

Let me attempt an answer by asking a question: Have you ever lived a single day without trust—a trust that carries on despite much doubt? For example, consider the trust necessary to drive your car on public highways. You count on other drivers staying on their side of the road and stopping at red lights and not sideswiping you on the freeway. You don't *know* this will happen; in fact, if you pay attention to news reports, you have good reason to wonder whether you will make it home alive. But you act on the basis of probabilities: it makes more sense to continue to trust and keep driving than to give in to doubt and stay where you are.

There is no end to the examples we could give. You trust your doctor (are you *certain* she's not a quack?). You board the airplane (are you *certain* the pilot hasn't been drinking?). You get married (are you *certain* this person won't become someone who makes your life miserable?). Or you get divorced (are you really *certain* your life will improve?).

Trust is a necessary part of life, and it always involves risk. Trust in God is no different. Given the suffering in this world, given the way things seem out of control, given the fact that God doesn't speak with an audible voice or appear in the same undeniable way in which you now see a book in your hands, trust in God always entails a certain amount of doubt. Personally, I consider it a good day if my certainties only slightly outnumber my doubts. Nonetheless, I've chosen to pack my camels and head west—to entrust my life to a God who loves me. There's nothing particularly pious about this; I merit no credit. It's just the most reasonable choice.

But, God knows, I sometimes see my belief as something praiseworthy that sets me apart from others. I never miss an opportunity to focus on myself, especially if there's an opportunity to pat myself on the back. The reason for this, of course, is my resistance to grace. I like to think that I am doing something to deserve God's blessing, that I am in some way—even a small way—contributing to my own salvation. So sometimes I turn faith into work (with plenty of sweating and straining) to protect myself from the full, loving onslaught of grace. My pride finds it hard to swallow undiluted mercy; instead my pride waters it down with nonsense about my own contributions and achievements.

This is nonsense because faith is the great antiwork. If you're being pulled back to shore by strong arms, do you take pride in your contribution to the rescue effort? After Paul wrote, "For by grace you have been saved through faith," he wanted to make sure his readers didn't misunderstand, so he immediately added, "and this is not your own doing; it is the gift of God—not the result of works, so that no one may boast."[5] Faith contributes not a whit to our salvation; it simply leans into the salvation God has already given us.

{ .. .. }

If we're afraid to lean that far, it may be because we've been disappointed by others. We live in a broken world, after all, filled with people like us: shortsighted, weak, and more than a little selfish. We've trusted before, but sometimes the trust has been misplaced.

When my daughter was a toddler and ready to start "potty training," I set her on the toilet. She said, "Daddy, you won't drop me, will you?"

"No, honey, I won't drop you," I assured her.

And then I dropped her. Her little body slipped right through my hands and splashed into the water. I can still see her terrified eyes accusing me over the rim of the seat. I pulled her out as quickly as I could and dried her off and told her that I would never, never, *never* drop her again. I knew enough Freudian psychology to keep me awake at night worrying about what I might have done to her.

She seems to have survived my clumsiness quite well, but she probably bears other scars of failed trust. We all do. Our parents, siblings, friends, and spouses have disappointed us in one way or another, and this has sometimes caused us to retreat into a castle of self-protection; we resolve to trust no one. But this never lasts long, for the undeniable reason that we *must* trust to get through life.

So not long after I failed my daughter, I rounded the corner from the hallway into the living room and heard a little voice say, "Daddy, catch!" I jerked around and saw her launch herself off the back of the couch, giggling as she flew through the air. I caught her, luckily. Even as I still remember the look on her face when I dropped her, I also remember the sound of her laughter in my arms. She trusted me fully, without reserve.

I can offer you no better image of biblical faith than this. We can throw ourselves at God with childlike abandon because of what we have seen in Jesus Christ. Perhaps you are hesitant because of past disappointments; perhaps you have doubts about God; perhaps you are just plain frightened. Well, I don't mean to sound uncaring, but honestly, your disappointments, doubts, and fears aren't so fascinating or significant. I recommend that you forget about yourself and all your reasons for not jumping, even forget about faith and whether you have it, and simply look at God—at the steadfast love that will never let you go—and maybe, without even noticing it, you'll slip off the back of the couch into very strong arms.

The years I spent in Scotland working on my Ph.D. at the University of Edinburgh were a great delight, not the least because I developed a close friendship with my supervisor, Alan Lewis. After I returned to the United States, Alan and I continued to talk with each other, usually over the telephone but sometimes (rarely) in person. One day he telephoned to say he had accepted a teaching position in Texas. This news caused great jubilation on both sides of the Atlantic, but the laughter stopped when he got the X-ray for his visa. It showed a large tumor growing between his heart and lungs.

He faced his sickness with great courage, deciding to follow through with his plans and resume his new duties. It wasn't easy. In addition to moving to a new culture and preparing for new classes, he had to undergo chemotherapy and its attendant sickness. But he persevered, thereby teaching his students much more than theology.

When he came near the end of life, I flew halfway across the country to be at his side. As I walked quietly into his hospital room, I saw his black hair splayed across the pillow, and his frail body barely discernible under the sheet, and intravenous needles pumping liquids into him and various monitors conveying information out of him, and a screen next to his bed that showed, with a wavy red line, every beat of his heart.

"Hello, Alan," I said.

As he lifted his heavy eyelids, his first words were, "Christ is victorious, and I know that I am not excluded but included in his victory. I have not felt despair. I've been confused, bewildered. But not in despair. The solid rock at the bottom is secure."

Part Three

Upside-Down Self

Chapter Ten

Set Free, Not Condemned

I ONCE HAD a professor say that whenever you see *therefore* in a text, you should ask what it's there for. If a writer is making a careful argument, leading readers from one point to the next, she uses *therefore* to signal a transition: "Here comes the logical conclusion, so pay close attention."

The Bible contains many *therefore*s (perhaps they should always be in italics), none more significant than the one Paul uses at the beginning of Romans 8. He has just shown how God dealt decisively with the problem of sin, offering Christ's righteousness as an atonement for our unrighteousness, and that this grace may be received not through works but through faith.

He has also acknowledged that this faith doesn't instantly deliver us from a continuing struggle with sin. "I do not understand my own actions," Paul confesses, using himself as an example. "For I do not do what I want, but I do the very thing I hate."[1] If he had such trouble, what chance do we have? Our pride, disobedience, and falsehood might have been effectively annulled through the incarnation, death, and resurrection of Jesus Christ, but every day, and often before we finish our second cup of coffee, we fall on our face despite our best intentions.

You want to start your day with prayer, say, but just as you get concentrated on God the neighbor's dog starts barking, which makes you recall its barking at midnight, which makes you want to shoot it, which makes you think that while you're at it, you'd like to smash the windows of the ugly car your neighbor always parks in front of your house, which makes you wonder how anyone so aesthetically challenged could have such a beautiful wife, which makes you wonder what she's doing at this very minute, which makes you imagine her in the shower . . . "Oh, yeah," you say to yourself, "I was supposed to be praying. Sorry, God."

Or you determine to be more gracious to your husband, but as you stagger out of bed you stumble over the sneakers he has once again left on the floor of the bathroom, which makes you recall how he never picks up after himself and yet expects you to keep the house spotlessly clean, which makes you think of the way he treats you, which makes you feel pretty sorry for yourself, which makes you respond to his inquiry about breakfast with "Who the hell cares?" Or something like that.

Or you promise to rely more fully on grace, to trust that God is good and loving, and not allow so many things to worry you. But as you walk outside to get the newspaper you remember the subscription bill is due, which reminds you that you must also pay both the Visa bill and the premium for your medical insurance before the end of the week, which makes you think of your nearly empty bank account, which sets your mind and stomach churning.

"For I do not do what I want, but I do the very thing I hate."

No matter how much you lean into God's grace and, in gratitude, want to be better person, self-centeredness keeps pulling you back to your old ways, keeps drawing you into your old patterns of behavior. So, just as you're ready to start believing that you're an especially egregious sinner, that you're nothing but dog meat in a world of prime rib, that you're totally, completely, and without qualification hopeless, the apostle transitions to a blessed *therefore:* "There is therefore now no condemnation for those who are in Christ Jesus."

No condemnation.

Not even a little bit.

None.

{ .. .. }

What the apostle meant, of course, is that there is no condemnation *from God.* As for condemnation from other sources, that's another matter.

Many of us—perhaps *most* of us at one time or another—have experienced condemnation from other people. It need not be explicit or even intentional; much of it comes disguised as caring love, honest concern, or upstanding morality.

Parents, for example, almost always intend the best for their children, but the intention can easily slide into ever-present criticism. "What, you got only a B in algebra?" "Thanks for making us breakfast, but we wish you would clean up after yourself." "The hit you got in the third inning was great, but you'd get more of them if you would just remember to keep your eye on the ball." Criticism, especially from those who care the most for us, can be a steady stream that, in time, erodes the rock of confidence.

Teachers and coaches, who should know better but are themselves flawed individuals, can do much harm. When I was in the second grade, my parents moved to another city, which meant I had to enter a new class in May. The only seat available was in the back, and being a little guy I had a hard time seeing. I was overwhelmed by everything and felt terribly alone. So I whispered something to a boy next to me. Unfortunately, the teacher happened to see me at that moment and called me to the front of the class. She announced my terrible crime, and then she grabbed my hand, turned over my palm, and whipped it with a ruler. That was my introduction to the class. I can still feel the burning shame.

A spouse, once the bloom of romance has wilted and the day-to-day challenges of living with another person have mounted, can take over from parents and teachers and subtly or not so subtly communicate that we're not what we advertised ourselves to be, that we're not as perfect we once seemed, that when it really gets down to it, we're *lacking.*

Even the institution that is supposed to manifest the acceptance of God—the church—can, in its zeal to uphold moral and spiritual standards, leave us feeling like scum of the earth. Preaching that constantly holds before us the ideal and sternly cracks the whip over us can make feel like lousy Christians.

When I was a pastor, I spoke with many who bore wounds of religious rejection. Some had been thrown out of congregations because of divorce; some had been chastised for not giving enough money; some had been abused as children; some had been told they hadn't been baptized properly; some had been made to believe they hadn't really received the Holy Spirit. They sought my counsel, partly to try to understand what had happened to them, but mostly, I think, to look into my eyes to see whether they saw any flicker of condemnation. I marvel at the courage this took.

You get walloped by condemnation whenever you're made to feel that you are not enough of something: not spiritual enough, or disciplined enough, or organized enough, or dedicated enough, or conservative enough, or liberal enough, or straight enough, or generous enough, or moral enough, or, well, you name it. When you're not enough of something, you know you don't belong. Condemnation sets you apart from those who are better; it exiles you for bad behavior.

Perhaps worse than the criticism we get from others is what we pile on ourselves. The two are connected, actually, because the latter often results from the former; we condemn ourselves because we've internalized the negative judgments of others, and thus we feel guilty or ashamed.

Many attempts have been made to differentiate guilt and shame. Lewis Smedes says guilt refers to what you do, and shame to who you are.[2] Some, following Freud, say guilt comes from internal criticism, and shame results from external disapproval.[3] But the more you read and think about it, the more the line blurs. For our purposes, the distinction is not important. Guilt or shame, you're seriously unhappy with yourself.

Two distinctions, however, are worth noting. First, there is a difference between objective and subjective guilt. If I've violated a law, whether civil or moral or spiritual, I'm guilty regardless of my feelings; when I drive ten miles per hour over the speed limit, I'm objectively at fault even if I don't happen to notice that I'm speeding and thus have no remorse over it. Subjective guilt, on the other hand, is the feeling of wrongdoing, which may or may not be based in objective fact.

This feeling, to make a further distinction, can be constructive or destructive. Not all guilt is bad, despite what you hear from pop psychologists. Being sorrowful over something we've done, or being ashamed of ourselves, may be entirely appropriate, if what we've done is actually wrong—provided it leads to a constructive end, such as making amends or changing our behavior. The capacity to feel guilt or shame indicates moral awareness. To use an extreme case, we would consider a murderer who shows no remorse to be either mentally ill or thoroughly evil.

But guilt is inappropriate when it turns inward. It becomes a destructive emotion, sometimes called "neurotic guilt," that is a form of self-punishment or even self-rejection. Instead of motivating us to become better people, it beats us down, makes us unable to rise up. This is what we get when we internalize the criticism of parents and others, and when we continually fail our best intentions and stumble through daily failures. We see ourselves as bad, and then we don't live up to our own best intentions, which confirms just how bad we really are . . . and thus we fall into a downward spiral.

{ .. .. }

The Bible certainly speaks about guilt, but of the three Greek words translated in that way not one refers to feelings. Instead, the words indicate our objective condition before God (we've all sinned), which has been overturned through Jesus Christ. Guilt, as far as the Bible is concerned, has significance only because it underscores the magnitude of God's grace. It is a thing of the past, the shadow that has been thoroughly vanquished by the Light that has come into the world.

What about feelings of guilt? At most, they serve only the temporary purpose of encouraging us to make amends if we have harmed others, and motivating us to flee to the embrace of grace. But this embrace smothers guilt. If God has overcome our guilt, what right do we have to wallow in it? Such self-condemnation is supremely pointless and an affront to God; to beat ourselves up is to pick a fight with God.

Thus we come again to our resistance to grace. Self-flagellation is a form of works, a way we try to atone for sin. If we punish ourselves enough, we think, we will make up for our failures; if we prove our desire to be a better person, God will be impressed with us.

So it's no wonder we internalize the criticism of others and condemn ourselves when we fail; by keeping the mud of guilt deep enough, we have something to *do,* some means of atonement. Besides, we've grown accustomed to it. Never underestimate the power of habit.

So what happens when we hear that there is *no condemnation* to those who are in Christ Jesus? Well, that's nice, thank you very much, but we'll keep supplying our own. We're like those prisoners we sometimes hear about who have grown so comfortable in confinement they don't want to leave. Some commit a crime immediately after their release to get sent back to the routine of punishment.

The good news of grace announces that the cell door has been thrown open so hard its hinges have broken. God does not condemn us, which makes condemnation from others (including ourselves) completely meaningless, if not nonsensical. God has set us free! Now, this freedom might threaten us, might make us afraid of leaving the familiar, might force us to adopt a new self-image.

But to be a free person! Our world suddenly becomes spacious, enabling us to stand up straight and breathe deeply and walk (or run!) forward into the life we were created to enjoy. Condemnation constricts, grace liberates.

{ .. .. }

One day Jesus was teaching in Jerusalem, according to the Gospel of John, and the scribes and Pharisees—the religious heavyweights—dragged a woman before Jesus. She had been caught in the very act of adultery, they told Jesus. The "very act" implies the presence of a man, does it not? Where was he? Probably at home telling his wife what a busy day he had at the office and thanking God for the blessings of a double standard.

"In the law," they said, "Moses commanded us to stone such women. Now what do you say?" They were testing Jesus. They had already condemned the woman, shaming her and threatening to kill her, but the reason they brought Jesus into it was to condemn him too. They were on a roll.

Of course, they began by quoting Scripture. Count on it: those who make it their business to expose the failures of others usually appeal to some higher authority to justify their actions. They don't want to be judgmental, after all, so they cover their shabby motives in piety, wanting to prove (most of all to themselves) that they're concerned only about upholding the highest standards, that they want only God's will (which always bears a close resemblance to their own). They take what was meant to be a source of life and turn it into a club of death. "But the Bible says . . ." "Doesn't the Law tell us . . . ?" "In chapter four, verse twelve . . ." When you hear things like this, cover your head, because stones are about to start flying.

Nothing fires up the spirit of condemnation quite as much as sex. Buried in the human unconscious is a cauldron of sexual longings, anxieties, fantasies, jealousies, and guilt—and catching an adulterer, well, that causes the pot to boil over. No one (with the possible exception of eunuchs) deals with sexual matters objectively. We all project our stuff onto others, especially those who might be getting away with something we secretly desire.

"What do you say, Jesus? Should we stone her?" It was a trap. How could Jesus deny the law without undermining the very thing he claimed to fulfill? How could he possibly explain away the clear teaching of Moses? ("Jesus, we've got just one word for you: Gotcha!")

But he played it cool and didn't say anything. He simply wrote something in the dust. Unfortunately, we don't know what it was. Curiosity would almost paralyze us at this point, if it weren't for what happened next: they kept pestering him with questions, until he finally stood up and said, "Let anyone among you who is without sin be the first to throw a stone at her." Then he bent down and resumed writing.

I imagine the scribes and Pharisees looking at each other for a few minutes, completely bewildered and befuddled. If I had been there, I would have signed up with Jesus on the spot. There's nothing quite so inspiring as seeing hypocrites laid low, unless you're the hypocrite.

Then they left. Not surprising, the elders were the first to go.

When Jesus and the woman were alone, he asked, "Has no one condemned you?"

"No one, sir."

"Neither do I condemn you. Go your way, and from now on do not sin again."[4]

The scribes and Pharisees *wanted* to condemn her; they wanted her to know just how bad she really was, how much she had failed, how unworthy she was even to live.

But Jesus, through cleverness and compassion, set her free.

Chapter Eleven

Life, Not Death

LET'S BEGIN THIS chapter where we ended the last one. The men who wanted to stone the adulteress were judgmental, self-righteous, cruel, and hypocritical. Not the sort of people you'd want to have over for dinner.

But they had a point.

We should try to understand it, distasteful as this might be. Their response was actually fitting, *given their view of reality.* They lived in a world of law, a world in which God's will was codified and sanctions were imposed, a world of cause and effect: obedience leads to blessing and disobedience to punishment, and the ultimate punishment is death. If you turn your back on the source of life, what are you facing? "The wages of sin is death."[1] To stone the woman would have been an unambiguous acting out of this logic.

The problem is, there weren't enough stones to go around. After they finished off the woman, they would have to heave stones at everyone else too, including each other. The last one standing, bruised and bloodied from the melee, would have to be crushed by a rock slide or by a boulder hurled from heaven. *Everyone* deserves the stoning—the woman, yes, and her partner, and even those who in indignant fury were ready to condemn her. "All have sinned and fall short of the glory of God."[2] No exceptions. Everyone has turned away from God and thus toward death.

But if everyone got what he or she deserved, if creation were to dissolve into death, God's purposes of love would be thwarted. So as we've seen, God deals with this dilemma through something that transcends logic, through the sublime gift of grace. In Jesus Christ, God entered our humanity, died for our sins, and opened the doors to eternal life. God's salvation overthrows the reign of death by the invasive, conquering power of eternal life.

Now, we should understand that when Scripture speaks about eternal life ("For God so loved the world that he gave his only Son, so that everyone who believes in him may not perish but have eternal life"[3]), it means something more than future life; it refers to a whole new dimension and quality of being, to be experienced now and forever. "I came," said Jesus, "that they may have life, and have it abundantly."

God's grace aims at this. Its chief purpose isn't to ease a guilty conscience, enhance self-esteem, curb destructive impulses, or foster spiritual ecstasy. It wants resurrection, the raising of the dead to new life.

{ .. .. }

Max De Pree has a granddaughter named Zoe, the Greek word for *life.* She was born prematurely and weighed one pound, seven ounces; she was so small that Max's wedding ring could slide up her arm to her shoulder. The neonatologist who first examined her said she had a 5–10 percent chance of living three days. To complicate matters, Zoe's biological father had jumped ship a few months earlier.

Dear Zoe is a collection of letters Max wrote to Zoe. Here is one of them:

> A wonderful thing happened to me a few days after you were born. We had scrubbed up carefully and put on the usual gown and mask. We were standing next to your isolette in the neonatal intensive care unit. You had two IVs in your navel, one in your foot, a monitor on each side of your chest, and a respirator tube and a feeding tube in your mouth.
>
> While we were looking at you, a wonderful nurse named Ruth came over to chat. After a few minutes she turned to me and said, "For the next several months, at least, you're the surrogate father. I want you to come to the hospital every day to visit Zoe, and when you come I would like you to rub her body and her legs and arms with the tip of your finger. While you're caressing her, you should tell her over and over how much you love her, because she has to be able to connect your voice to your touch."
>
> I'm sure Ruth's suggestion is going to be very important in our relationship together. I also have the feeling that she has given me something enormously profound to ponder.[4]

De Pree's voice and touch helped bring Zoe into being. God's voice and touch in Jesus Christ, the Word made flesh, says, "I love you, I love you, I love," until *zoe*—life—comes to be.

Ireneus, the great second-century theologian, said, "The glory of God is a man fully alive." What he meant, I think, is that the beauty and power of God becomes ever more evident as we awaken to the life we were meant to enjoy. God wants us to thrive as human beings, to fulfill our potential as bearers of the divine image.

But this is not the impression you get from some of God's press secretaries. Their news briefings are often negative: don't do that, curb your appetites, reign in desire, discipline and sacrifice yourself. They make it seem that the goal of God's administration is to shut down human life, to narrow and constrict it; they imply that God's most important word to us is *no!*

Self-denial has its place, but only as a means to another end. Jesus said that his followers must deny themselves *in order to* save themselves; they must take up their own cross as a way to gain life.[5] Sacrifice, which may be necessary in our broken world, is not the purpose of our existence. We were made for the blessings on the other side of sacrifice; we were made for life, not death.

{ .. .. }

What does it mean to be fully alive?

Remember, the abundant life comes through resurrection. It's the creation of something that, strictly speaking, is without analogy. We cannot conceive of it until it happens. Like those who wanted to stone the adulteress, we're still shaped by the old reality, the world of law and sin and death. Our imagination is too crippled to walk into a new land. But once in a while, even in our broken, death-marked existence, we experience it, unexpectedly and with a force that pulls us out of the grave.

It happened to me last Saturday. The preceding weeks were difficult, with disappointment accumulating and resentment growing; my little world felt dark, lonely, and abandoned by God. Late in the morning, after visiting a friend in a nursing home, I decided to go for a long run and walk along the beach, something I hadn't done for a while.

After about fifteen minutes, I became intensely aware of my surroundings: the shades of blue in sky and sea, the waves breaking and the gulls bickering, the smells of wet sand and salty air and suntan lotion, and above it all the pelicans soaring. The spring day was as fresh and pure as a child's laughter. Then I felt myself laughing, at nothing in particular but everything in general. I realized I had been lifted above my pain; for the moment at least, the broken pieces of my heart were pieced together into a new wholeness.

Several times I stopped and looked out toward the distant horizon line. I breathed deeply, greedily gulping in as much air as I could. I wasn't winded from my run; I had no biological need for more oxygen. But I felt liberated from the narrow confinement of self-preoccupation and delivered into a broad spaciousness. I was breathing in the manner of a trapped miner who has just been rescued, or a drowning person pulled ashore by a lifeguard. It was as though I wanted to take the spaciousness into myself even as I was entrusted to it.

When I began to pray, I quickly lost interest in my list of requests. To ask for anything seemed inappropriate, even greedy. I wanted only to say, "Thank you, thank you, thank you." What I was experiencing, it occurred to me, was an odd contentment.

I was at the beach for about two hours, or so my watch indicated. But it could have been two minutes or two days; my experience seemed timeless, as though it were part of something that couldn't be measured. I was not in ecstasy, in the sense of standing outside myself; rather, I seemed to be standing more fully within myself, within the self I was created to be.

Healing, spaciousness, gratitude—these, I believe, are some of the gifts of resurrection. As sinners jostling against other sinners, we have plenty of open wounds, bleeding and raw, and we need healing not just from death's final blow but from all its preliminary incursions. To become fully alive, we have to be delivered from the self-centeredness that has cramped us and thus stunted our growth; we have to be turned outward toward a spaciousness large enough to include God, other people, and the world around us. Surely, being healed and turned inside out fills us with a thanksgiving that springs from a deep and sustained contentment—a contentment, moreover, that comes when restless longing is swallowed up in fulfillment.

{ .. .. }

We must make an important distinction: resurrection has nothing to do with the immortality of the soul. To believe the latter (quoting Frederick Buechner) "is to believe that though John Brown's body lies a-mouldering in the grave, his soul goes marching on simply because marching on is the nature of souls just the way producing apples is the nature of apple trees. Bodies die, but souls don't."[6] This idea affords us great comfort, especially when a loved one dies, and it's been an immensely popular belief. Funeral sermons are constantly assuring us that although Uncle Bob's body lies in a coffin, he himself is alive and well, happy to be delivered from the prison of his flesh.

There are two problems with this: it's an idea imported from Greek philosophy, and it's not found in the Bible. The writers of Scripture assume a unity of the person; body and soul cannot be separated but are intricately interwoven. I do not *have* a body, I *am* a body. When my body dies, I will not live on happily ever after; I will be as dead as the proverbial doornail. The news in Jesus Christ is of resurrection, the re-creation of new life out of the nothing of death. Resurrection happens to the whole person, and that's why the creed affirms "the resurrection of the body and the life everlasting." The Christian hope for Uncle Bob is that one day, body and soul, he will rise dancing out of the grave.

Perhaps one reason belief in the immortality of the soul is so widespread is its implication that within each of us is something eternal, a divine spark simply needing to be fanned into flame. Life is already buried within, it tells us, and all we have to do is nurture and release it. So we should step up the pace of our prayers; we should spend more time in meditation, fasting, or other spiritual disciplines.

The immortality of the soul, in other words, is a way to protect ourselves from the radical nature of grace; it's a way to tame grace by turning it into a form of assistance. Grace as personal trainer. Grace as advice and encouragement. But as we've seen, the grace revealed in Jesus Christ is not a coach but a creator: it makes a new Adam or a new Eve out of dust.

So there is the only son of a widow, dead and on his way to burial, with a great crowd of mourners weeping and wailing, and Jesus stops the procession, places his hand on the bier, and says, "Young man, I say to you, rise!" And the corpse gets up.[7]

There is the daughter of Jairus, a leader of the synagogue, who died in her home—a home now filled with the commotion of grief, as relatives and neighbors give vent to despair—and Jesus takes her by the hand and says, "*Talitha cum,*" which means, "Little girl, get up!" And the corpse gets up.[8]

There is Lazarus, four days in the tomb, his sisters in anguish and the townsfolk gathered to comfort with casseroles, hugs, and tender silences, and Jesus issues a loud command—"Lazarus, come out!" And the corpse gets up.[9]

The one who himself was raised from the dead—Jesus the Christ—is the embodiment of God's grace; thus in his presence corpses can't stay down for long. Death doesn't stand a chance around abundant life.

"If anyone is in Christ," Paul told the Corinthians, "there is a new creation: everything old has passed away; see! everything has become new!"[10] This is because Christ is "the resurrection and the life,"[11] he who heals our wounds, turns us toward God, and fills us with a peace that passes all understanding. The final resurrection will happen in the future, when our broken bodies and souls are refashioned into something wholly new; but it also happens, preliminarily and partially, in the present, in those unexpected experiences, such as I had at the beach, that lift us and enable us to become more fully alive.

Chapter Twelve

Death, Not Life

IF THE ARC of God's salvation leads to an empty tomb, if the goal of God's grace is resurrection, then we're compelled to acknowledge an obvious but nonetheless shocking fact: *the only requirement for resurrection is death.*

Jesus didn't come to repair the repairable or amend the amendable. He came to raise the dead; he came to create life *ex nihilo,* out of nothing. He always does his best work in the presence of death, literal and metaphorical. By the latter, I mean those intimations of nothingness where death is already dissolving holes in the fabric of our being through weakness, defeat, suffering, grief, and despair. The parts of our lives that cause fear and shame are precisely where Jesus gets busy and shows his stuff.

When Mary and Martha asked him to come heal their brother, what did Jesus do? He stayed put. He waited until Lazarus had died, been wrapped in grave clothes, and buried four days; then, when there was no doubt that death and death alone was all Jesus had to work with, he showed up and spoke life-giving words to the corpse.

I like to imagine Lazarus a few years later, after Jesus himself was raised from death and a new movement was being started in his name. The religion editor of the *Jerusalem Times* is interviewing him:

> "Lazarus, you've become an important symbol in this new Jesus movement. What accounts for your influence?"
>
> "Beats me."
>
> "Well, your modesty is charming, but seriously, there must be some reason. What has been your most important ministry?"
>
> "I died."
>
> "Yes, but you must have had great faith or hope."
>
> "No. Dead people don't have faith or hope."
>
> "But you must have done *something* right."
>
> "What is it about 'dead' you don't understand? The only thing I did was what corpses do: not a damn thing! Excuse my language, but I'm tired of explaining this. I was nothing. *Nothing.* And then somehow, some way, I became a new something."

Grace loves to operate, in other words, when there can be no doubt that it's doing everything. Salvation is not a cooperative venture, wherein God lends a helping hand to assist our latent potential. No, God does *all* the heavy lifting. Grace bestows riches on those who don't have two cents to their name. "Blessed are the poor in spirit," Jesus said.

Which leaves us in an awkward situation. The thing we most fear, death in all its forms, now yields the possibility for the thing we most want, life in all its fullness. As Ernest Becker has argued so persuasively, we shape our personality—from neurotic self-defense to heroic achievement—with a single, largely unconscious, goal: to deny the terror of death.[1] We struggle for success and security to protect ourselves against the threat of nothingness. The light of Jesus' resurrection, though, reveals something so startling we can scarcely comprehend it: our nothingness is precisely what God finds most useful in our lives.

The Apostle Paul told the Corinthians about a time he was nearly paralyzed by depression: "We were so utterly, unbearably crushed that we despaired of life itself. Indeed, we felt that we had received the sentence of death so that we would rely not on ourselves but on God who raises the dead."[2] When you're lying in a cold, dark tomb, you're not reading the Bible or going to church, you're not praying and meditating, you're not chanting or filling your mind with positive thoughts—you're not doing anything, which is another way of saying that you're *absolutely* dependent on God who raises the dead. You have no choice but to trust grace.

{ .. .. }

The reason death is not the bad news we feared is because it has already been taken up into the death of Jesus. Our death has become his death. This means his resurrection will be our resurrection; his life will be our life.

Robert Capon is an Episcopal priest and a fine New Testament scholar. Despite his religious vocation, he never felt much personal enthusiasm over what God had done for him in Jesus. Why? "Well," he explains, "I now think it was because I believed, back then, that I wasn't broken enough to need fixing." That changed when he had an adulterous affair. He confessed to his wife of twenty-four years, who refused to give him another chance and ended the marriage.

Capon's initial reaction to this turn of events was denial (it couldn't be happening) and anger ("she had to forgive me, dammit!"). These were attempts, he eventually realized, to regain *control* of the situation, to get his life back to where it belonged, with him in the driver's seat. He writes:

> But then it slowly began to dawn on me that my control wasn't going to come back: I was going to have to face something I'd never seriously faced before: the fact that I was *powerless.* None of the devices I tried to use on her did any good. My control hadn't slipped; it was gone. But in the end—and with me fighting the realization every inch of the way—the truth came to me: it wasn't that I was powerless, or out of control, or unhappy, or hurt. I was *dead.* I had no more influence than a corpse over my own life. . . .
>
> It was a distinctly bush-league death. But it was the first death I'd ever had, and it was enough for God to get me to welcome the Passion back into my life. So if God doesn't balk at the quality of anyone's death (the church's 2,000-year-long fuss over suicides notwithstanding), you shouldn't balk at mine. Besides, it was *my* death. I, who had spent fifty years trying to convince everybody (myself included) that

> I was *something else,* had ended up as nothing whatsoever. Not as guilty, or as a sinner, or as a basket case; but as zero. Yet suddenly, by the grace of God, every light in the New Testament went on, and everything that the church had in her basement of belief hit me like a cask-strength, single-malt Scotch: *This was where I had been all along!* I didn't have to get over my death; I had only to be *in it*—because that was where Jesus my life was. I developed, in short, a passion for the Passion.[3]

We do not have to get over our death, much less deny it, because this is where we meet the source of new life. Jesus finds us in the tomb, buried in fear, weakness, doubt, and much failure, and he says, "Lazarus, come out!" We're as shocked as anyone. We were hoping to restore ourselves to be of use to God; hoping to be courageous and strong, to have faith and do *something* right. We not only hoped for these things, we tried with all our might to pull it off. That we never succeeded only made us work all the harder, pumping ourselves up with the dominant American philosophy—the power of positive thinking—and telling ourselves that if we just gave it a little more sweat and strain we'd eventually get ourselves in reasonably good shape. This required a prodigious amount of deception, of course; we became spin masters to evade the truth that we were already sinking faster than concrete blocks in the River Styx.

Now, when we can no longer deceive ourselves or anyone else, when we haven't the energy—physical, mental, spiritual—

to do anything except acknowledge that we're dead, that it's all over, kaput, *the end,* then Jesus meets us with a commission.

{ .. .. }

Bob Blackford and I have been friends for many years. He married a childhood friend of mine, Joanne, and enrolled in the seminary where I was a student. Bob and Joanne even moved next door to my wife and me. After graduation, though, our conversation became infrequent, largely because we were both busy juggling the demands of being husbands, fathers, and Christian leaders.

When I received news of his being diagnosed HIV-positive as a consequence of a homosexual affair, I was as stunned as the rest of his friends. In those days, it was an automatic sentence of death, which is what we all—including Bob—expected. He assumed his life was over, and in way it was. Although Joanne graciously forgave him, their marriage would never be the same; he suffered painful tension with his two daughters; he lost his standing in the community; he underwent a devastating blow to his self-worth. As AIDS waged war on his immune system, Bob entered a constant quest for the right combination of drugs and a struggle to maintain his T cells.

Bob had no choice but to be in his death. There was no escaping who he was or what he had done; there was no denying that he was a dead man walking.

Then a strange thing happened on the way to the grave. He met Jesus anew, and the One who is the resurrection and the life decided that Bob was now broken enough, *nothing enough,* to become really useful. It didn't happen quickly. Slowly, a window of opportunity opened here, and a door flung open there; far from dying Bob started living with more vitality—at least of the spiritual sort—than ever before. To be sure, he is still battling the disease; some days he feels weak, and he has no idea how many years are ahead of him. He hardly has time to worry about it, though, because God has given him and Joanne work to do—in Africa, it turns out. They have recently spoken to thousands of people in Nigeria, South Africa, and Kenya; they have met with AIDS patients, led pastors' conferences, preached in churches, and been interviewed on television. Most of all, they have witnessed to the redemptive power of Jesus Christ.

Bob wouldn't want you to think of him as a spiritual hero. No one has noticed a halo over his head; he still struggles with fear and temptation and doubt. He's still a sinner, in other words, just like everyone else. But it's precisely sinners that God has a thing for, and the deader the better; so Jesus met Bob in his death and his grave has become a gateway to life.[4]

{ .. .. }

The abundant life God intends for us comes not because we lift ourselves by our own bootstraps. This has always been an impossibility, despite its honored place in American mythology. Resurrection happens when we're dead (unable to lift a finger, let alone our bootstraps), because the motivating power behind it is grace—God's free decision to be for us, to rebuild our broken lives, to remake us from the dust of nothingness.

Chapter Thirteen

Truth, Not Evasion

YOU CAN'T EMBARRASS a corpse.

The dead are not threatened by anything, least of all the truth. They no longer have to contend with pride or worry about image. What sense would it make to puff up nothingness? A billion times zero is still zero. And that's OK—more than OK, it's spectacularly wonderful—because in the crazy math of the rule-breaking God, zeros are the only thing that add up to anything.

If God's grace is for those who have taken a nose dive into nothingness, why should they pretend they're still flying high? Grace is for those who know they can't rely on merit badges; grace is for those who don't have strength enough to give it one more try; grace is for those who have given up on themselves. Grace-saved people have nothing to hide. They enjoy the freedom of honesty.

Few burdens are more onerous than pretense: convincing the world (and most of all yourself) that you're socially respectable, morally upright, and spiritually mature is like carrying a hundred pounds of manure on your back; the whole load stinks to high heaven, but the fumes have so distorted your thinking that you're afraid to set it down for fear no one will like you. Once the strong arm of grace relieves you of the weight of self-justification, you feel like dancing—and others aren't afraid to dance with you.

Søren Kierkegaard wrote something to the effect that it's a consolation always to be in the wrong. I was thinking about this the other day when I decided to quit arguing with my wife about whether or not I listen to her. "You're right, sweetheart, I don't always listen. Sorry." It's amazing how that takes the steam out of a fight. With nothing to lose, you have everything to gain. But when you think you have something to lose, when you mount a spirited defense, you have nothing to gain: the enterprise ends in defeat, for the harder you work at defending yourself the guiltier you appear, which only makes you try all the harder . . . That's why it's a relief to admit that you're so far in debt you have to declare bankruptcy.

{ .. .. }

Why, then, are we reluctant to admit this?

The answer has to do with the central pretense of our lives: our denial of death. Ernest Becker, in his extraordinary synthesis of twentieth-century psychology, showed that our deepest unconscious energy is dedicated to protecting ourselves from our vulnerability to death. This is the source of both our neuroses (mechanisms of defense) and our achievements (grasping at transcendence). We do everything we can to keep the impending nothingness from touching the emotional center of our being.

To acknowledge minor failure is to acknowledge vulnerability to the major terror: if I'm guilty of a moral lapse, say, I have lost control of a part of my life, and this implies that I could lose control of my whole life, which is another way of saying I could die. From this terror, I expend all my energy to build a shield. So, admit I've done something wrong? No way! Admit that I'm a dead man walking, that I already have a foot in the grave, that I'm already up to my neck in nothingness? Not a chance.

That's why Becker, despite his brilliant analysis of our predicament, fails to help us in the end. In his final chapter, he is able only to admonish us to take life seriously, which means this: "Whatever man does on this planet has to be done in the lived truth of the terror of creation, of the grotesque, of the rumble of panic underneath everything."[1]

Excuse me, Professor Becker. You've just spent 280 pages convincing me that my whole life has been shaped around denying this "terror of creation." What makes you think I can suddenly change and live in the truth of it? What insight, however profound, can liberate me from decades of practiced deceit?

Our only hope is the resurrection of Jesus Christ. This assuages our deepest fear, for contrary to the evidence around us and in us we're destined for an existence that transcends death. But the resurrection questions our whole being too, because if this is what we need, we're creatures of death. In other words, we're completely vulnerable and dependent on grace.

How do we know this? The light of grace shining from the empty tomb tells us. As we've seen before, the order of events is important: we do not first admit our need and then search for something or someone to save us; instead, we are first seized by grace, startled by the truth that God loves us and destines us for resurrection, and only then do we find the freedom to admit our true situation.

Christian tradition calls this admission "confession of sin"; most often, it has about it a dull matter-of-factness. God's amazing grace reveals that I'm an amazing sinner; first-class mercy indicates a first-class screw-up. Yep, that's who I am. But having admitted this basic truth—and thus having no difficulty owning my little day-to-day failures—I have no need to carry on about it. Why should I torment myself with guilt if God has already dealt with it? Why should I be embarrassed about the stink of death clinging to me if God has already said, "Unbind him, and let him go!"? Genuine confession of sin, which happens in the freedom of grace, has little to do with breast-beating self-flagellation.

We should not minimize the seriousness of human failure; God went to considerable trouble to save us from its consequences. Nonetheless, from the advantage of our post-Easter perspective, *our sins and the death they deserve are inconsequential, hardly worth mentioning.*

{ .. .. }

That we do mention them is itself a gift. God's grace, as we have seen, is an embrace of love, a commitment to grow us into people who are fully alive. We cannot experience fully the abundant life until we dedicate ourselves to the truth—

the truth about God, first, and then the truth about ourselves and the world. Many of our problems, the things that beat us down and rob us of our humanity, are a consequence of our ceaseless and creative attempts to evade the truth.

M. Scott Peck in his best-selling book *The Road Less Traveled* says that what we need is "dedication to reality." Our neuroses and our character disorders result from suppressing the truth or taking shortcuts around it:

> Truth or reality is avoided when it is painful. We can revise our maps only when we have the discipline to overcome that pain. To have such discipline, we must be totally dedicated to truth. That is to say that we must always hold truth, as best we can determine it, to be more important, more vital to our self-interest, than our comfort. Conversely, we must always consider our personal discomfort relatively unimportant and, indeed, even welcome it in the service of the search for truth. Mental health is an ongoing process of dedication to reality at all costs.[2]

The cost for dedication to reality is very high, but God in Christ has paid the price, and now we have the freedom to affirm the truth about ourselves, no matter how painful it might be.

Since we have been claimed by grace, chosen not because of who we are or what we've done, we have no difficulty facing the harshest truth about ourselves: we're often selfish creatures, captive to an egocentrism that prevents us from loving God and other people in anything but a half-hearted way, and this leads us into uncountable wrongs, from minor peccadilloes to major failures.

But you would be perfectly right to yawn and say to me, "Well, yes, we're sinners. Now tell us something interesting."

All right, here it is: *the grace that reveals sin also confers inestimable worth.* This is the kicker, and it's a big one. Just when grace frees us to confess that we're sinners, it lifts us to a status higher than the angels. Just when grace enables us to acknowledge our nothingness, it announces that we're worth more than we can imagine because we're the beloved children of God. Just when grace forces us to look directly into the pale eyes of death, it assures us that we've been destined for resurrection.

Do you know who you really are? You're the one for whom God expended incomprehensible effort to embrace in love. You're the one for whom God became human to forgive your sin and defeat your death. All this was done, as I say, not just for the world in general but *for you* in particular. Of course you're a sinner. But please understand: this is significant only because it underscores the radical nature of grace, only because it proves God's extreme commitment to you, only because it leaves no doubt about just how valuable you really are.

A few years ago my state (in an act that seemed so *California*) established a commission to promote self-esteem. We have an insatiable desire to lead the nation in anything involving pop culture, including pop psychology, with the inevitable result that many things do not pop but instead fizzle. In the case of self-esteem, I doubt our tax dollars actually lifted anyone's, other than those who were appointed by the governor to serve on the commission. It was well intentioned, I suppose, but our politicians demonstrated a world-class naïveté in supposing a commission could do anything to promote it. The truth is, although humans can destroy self-esteem they have only limited and short-term power to rebuild it. The darkness and death that haunt us are far too destructive of our well-being to be overcome by human affirmation and encouragement, however important they might be. We need something stronger, something able to dispel darkness and triumph over death. We need nothing less than our Creator's love.

That's what we've received, and thus the truth about us, the reality to which we must be dedicated is this: we are sinners, up to our neck in the mud of nothingness; but grace lifts us, washes us off, and declares us beautiful, eternally valuable, and worthy of God's love.

Chapter Fourteen

Delight, Not Manipulation

AFTER THE RELIGIOUS dust settles, and after sermons have been delivered and theological tomes pondered and spiritual techniques practiced, we have a fundamental choice: we can relate to God with delight or with manipulation.

The latter is more popular, because it's consistent with the world we know so well, the world of cause and effect, the world of law and consequence. This approach logically assumes that if you want something good, you must earn it. Underlying this assumption is another one: God needs to be changed in some way; God needs to be convinced of our worthiness, or cajoled to bless us, or persuaded to act in a certain way. On these assumptions, large edifices of spirituality can be built. Daily prayer and Bible reading, church attendance and tithing, volunteer service and serious efforts to love—all can derive from the (usually unacknowledged) attempt to manipulate God into being more favorable toward us.

But when the disorienting grace of God finally sets reality before us, or perhaps more accurately drops us inescapably into the middle of reality, the dominant aspect of our relationship with God becomes delight. Well, why not? God, we discover, is not a deity to be feared or placated, but one who loves us and who has already embraced us in grace. We can trust this God, as we've seen, and once we entrust ourselves to God there is really not much left for us to *do,* except to delight.

The chief end of our lives becomes the Chief End. "What is the chief end of man?" the Shorter Catechism asks, and the answer is, "The chief end of man is to glorify God and to enjoy him forever." What does it mean to enjoy God? It means to worship and obey, without using these activities to haggle for God's blessing.

Worship and obedience, if I may venture a bold analogy, are not unlike sex. We would think poorly of anyone who uses sex as a bargaining chip, as a way to get something from another person. We have a name for this: prostitution. But where there is deep delight, where mutual love is the context, sex is a wonderful means of expression, a way to make explicit what one feels. So also are worship and obedience.

{ .. .. }

To understand worship, we need to go back to the beginning, to the thwarting of God's original intention. Donald Baillie, the great Scottish theologian, offers a memorable image of what went wrong, "a tale of God calling His human children to form a great circle for the playing of His game":

> In that circle we ought all to be standing, linked together with lovingly joined hands, facing towards the Light at the centre, which is God ("the Love that moves the sun and the other stars"); seeing our fellow creatures all round the circle in the light of that central Love, which shines on them and beautifies their faces; and joining with them in the dance of God's great game, the rhythm of love universal. But instead of that, we have, each one, turned our backs upon God and the circle of our fellows, and faced the other way, so that we can see neither the Light at the centre nor the faces on the circumference. And indeed in that position it is difficult even to join hands with our fellows! Therefore instead of playing God's game we play, each one, our own selfish little game. . . . Each one of us wishes to be the centre, and there is blind confusion, and not even any true *knowledge* of God or of our neighbors. That is what is wrong. . . .[1]

This is the legacy of sin: we have all wanted to play our own game, and in turning away from God we are no longer able see each other or hold each other's hands, and the shadows in front of us mock our every move. The game has stopped, and there is only blind confusion.

But in Christ, God has startled us with grace. The power of this amazement is such that it turns us back toward the center. Now, having been delivered from our pathetic, solitary dance, we happily join hands with our brothers and sisters, whose faces we see, and together we move to the rhythm of love. Although in one sense this is our duty, to name it such is misleading. It may be a husband's duty to make love to his wife, but who would think of it as anything but delight? When duty and delight wed, the union is supreme joy.

We gather to worship, usually on Sunday mornings, not because we can do this only once a week in a church building but to bear witness to what is true in all times and places, to make explicit that God is our constant delight and that we want to join the dance. First Baptist or St. Timothy's Catholic should probably be called Fellowship of the Rumba or Community of the Reel. My own tradition, in distrust and distaste of emotionalism, prides itself on taking seriously Paul's admonition to do things "decently and in order," but unless there is something slightly indecent and disorderly about our worship we might well wonder if we've missed the point. To worship is to give way to an adoration that arises spontaneously from delight. The arrangement of the elements of worship—prayer, praise in song, confession of sin, reading and proclamation of the Word, celebration of the sacraments—are the agreed-on steps in the dance, the way the community turns toward the Light at the center and organizes its joy.

My wife and I recently joined friends for coffee and dessert at a hotel. Walking to the outdoor dining patio, we were drawn to a large room, from which we heard music and much laughter. It turned out to be an anniversary celebration of a Lebanese couple. On one side of the room people sat bunched in conversation around tables, and on the other side dancers were linked with arms around shoulders, forming a circle around a drummer who beat out the rhythm. They took a few steps to the left, kicked their feet in front of them, and then steps to the right, and so on—a dance that was not invented ad hoc but was part of their culture. This shared form, far from constricting joy, made possible its expression; their delight was so attractive, so *catching*, that we couldn't keep from bouncing to the beat of the music as we stood in the doorway. My wife said, "I want to join them," and we were seriously tempted to crash the party.

The church's liturgical patterns, growing out of traditions and cultures, are meant to aid the delight, to make possible the community's celebration. If passers-by aren't attracted to the joy of the dance, it may be because the spirit of celebration has been lost and all that remains is the form.

{ .. .. }

Obedience, too, is an expression of delight. The psalmist prayed, "I delight to do your will, O my God; your law is within my heart."[2] We can pray something like this—and mean it—if we trust the goodness of God; we can *enjoy* God's will if we believe it leads to something good. Without this trust, God's will becomes a burdensome obligation (we must do it to stay out of trouble) and a means of manipulation (if we perform it well, we might convince God that we should be blessed). But in the light of grace, we see the law itself as a gift, an opportunity to demonstrate our desires.

In a loveless marriage, a wedding anniversary is an awkward, legalistic burden. Something must be done; you fear you'll be judged on whether you've taken the time to get a card and come up with a gift. You don't want to get in trouble, and you'd like to make your spouse happy enough to avoid unnecessary conflict. Under such circumstances, standing at the card rack is no delight. What a difference if you're in love: then the anniversary is an opportunity to express your feelings. The duty to buy a card and gift remains, but duty and delight are one.

This is the only way to make sense of Psalm 119, a huge (176 verses) meditation on the law. The psalmist who wrote it was besotted with affection for God's will. "I delight in the way of your decrees. . . . I will delight in your statutes. . . . Your decrees are my delight. . . . Your commandments are my delight. . . . Your law is my delight."[3] This from someone who had not yet seen the height, depth, and breadth of God's grace in Jesus Christ! How much more will those who have seen it rejoice in the opportunity the law affords. This does not mean that grace turns us back to legalism; grace always aims for freedom and works for wholeness. Should the law once again revert to its old ways, insinuating itself between God and us as a manipulative tool, grace will turn judgment and wrath upon it. But so long as the law stays in the proper place, it can be used to facilitate the dance. When we realize that we too have been delivered from slavery, just as the Israelites were set free from Egyptian bondage, we approach the Ten Commandments with interest: this is the will of the God who has saved us, and this is the way liberated people carry on with their lives. We're especially interested in what the embodiment of grace—

Jesus Christ—taught his disciples. His two great commandments (to love God with our whole being, and to love our neighbors as ourselves) and his Sermon on the Mount become our "law," the way our delight fleshes itself out in day-to-day living.

A person set free from the necessity to earn God's blessing desires, out of gratitude, to be a blessing; a person who does not have to do anything to receive God's love wants to do everything possible to return that love.

Charles Wesley, in his great hymn "Love Divine, All Loves Excelling," focused his imagining eye on heaven: "Let us see thy great salvation / Perfectly restored in Thee; / Changed from glory into glory, / Till in heaven we take our place, / Till we cast our crowns before Thee, / Lost in wonder, love, and praise." This is the Great Dance, the giving and receiving and giving back again, moving to the beat of Love Eternal. Having been restored and changed from glory into glory, we will throw all things back to the Creator in gratitude, even our rewards.

{ .. .. }

Finally, as we delight in God, we learn to delight in things that delight God.

Because I love my wife and she loves me, I look with favor on things that give her pleasure. I may not be naturally inclined toward beautiful plates and vases, for example, but she is, so I've started noticing them. A few days ago, as we were strolling through an art fair, I heard myself say, "Hey sweetheart, look at these beautiful plates!" At a much more important level, when I married her I married into a family; her mother became my mother-in-law, and her children became my stepchildren. In a sense, they were strangers to my affections. But as I have witnessed Shari's love for them, my own love has grown, and as grandchildren have arrived they have become my grandchildren as well. Yesterday, Shari and I were on the floor with little Kelsey, and I realized that I was enjoying Shari's delight as much as Kelsey herself—and yet, because of that delight, I too love Kelsey.

In a similar way, as we delight in God, we will of course turn our attention toward the objects of God's delight. God's passions become our passions. We too appreciate creation and begin to care for it, knowing it's the handiwork of God; most especially, we delight in that part of creation that bears God's own image, human beings.

In our neighborhood lives a retarded man who frequently walks his dog. He's friendly and very talkative; he'll give you the details of his parents' latest home improvement project, the itinerary of the neighbor's vacation, and a report on the latest model car he's building. The other day I was in a hurry and, frankly, just didn't want to talk with him. So when I saw him round the corner by our house, I ducked into our garage. As I stood skulking in the shadows, ashamed of myself, it occurred to me that God didn't treat me that way, and God didn't treat him that way either; God, in fact, was taking great delight in him that very minute.

Delight, Not Manipulation

I wish I could report that I immediately ran out to greet him. By the time I worked this through in my mind, however, he had already walked by our house, and I wasn't convicted enough to run after him.

God doesn't need to be convicted to run after anyone, which is why Francis Thompson called God "the Hound of Heaven." A hound on the chase may well be the perfect image of delight; if we delight in the Hound, we'll start running for all we're worth in the same direction.

Chapter Fifteen

Giving, Not Getting

WE LIVE IN what has often been called a consumerist culture, and we're constantly admonished to do our part. We're told we need a better house, a bigger SUV, a smaller cell phone, a sexier cologne, a snazzier watch, a faster computer. A few years ago, the *New York Times* estimated that the average American is exposed to thirty-five hundred advertisements a day.[1] Buy, buy, buy, we're told, and what we end up buying is the idea that the measure of our lives is how much we own.

The philosopher William James said, "A man's Self is the sum total of all that he can call his." Whether or not we've consciously endorsed this view, we live as if it's true. We believe we *are* what we *own.* Therefore we should do all we can to get, and get more.

But Jesus said, "Take care! Be on your guard against all kind of greed; for one's life does not consist in the abundance of possessions."[2] Then he told a story (as he often did to illustrate the point): "The land of a rich man produced abundantly. And he thought to himself, 'What should I do, for I have no place to store my crops?' Then he said, 'I will do this:

I will pull down my barns and build larger ones, and there I will store all my grain and my goods. And I will say to my soul, "Soul, you have ample goods laid up for many years; relax, eat, drink, be merry." ' "[3]

You have to like this guy. He would be honored by his state's agricultural commission, if not invited to the White House to be celebrated as Outstanding Farmer of the Year. He was *industrious.* He didn't achieve his success by drinking margaritas in the shade. He wasn't afraid to get dirt under his fingernails; he was in the fields before sunup and worked on his books long after the rest of the household had gone to sleep. He was also *progressive.* Not content with the status quo, he read farming journals and attended agricultural conventions, keeping up with the latest developments in harvest equipment and barn construction. Rather than have his land underproduce or his crops rot, he determined to build larger barns. His neighbors would soon be doing so, and if he didn't keep up with the times he'd be hurting. He was a *planner* too. Retirement wasn't far down the road, so he wanted to invest his resources in a way that would enable him to enjoy those years without being a burden on others. His financial planner helped him map out a strategy: buy more land, invest in bigger barns before his neighbors did, keep the price of wheat up by not flooding the market, and so on. We understand this guy. Industrious, progressive, a planner—what's not to like about him? He would make a great American, with just the sort of scrappy initiative we admire.

The rest of Jesus' story comes as a shock: "God said to him, 'You fool! This very night your life is being demanded of you. And the things you have prepared, whose will they be?' So it is with those who store up treasures for themselves but are not rich toward God."

As with many of his parables, Jesus leaves us wondering and pondering, and maybe a little perplexed. We would call this farmer wise. Why did God call him a fool?

Perhaps it was because he confused the means of life with the end of life, crossing over the line from living *by* his wealth to living *for* his wealth. Or perhaps he planned for the future but neglected eternity, forgetting that the angel of death would eventually separate him from his precious things. Or perhaps he thought he *was* what he *had,* imagining he was the sum total of all that he could call his.

"One's life does not consist in the abundance of possessions," Jesus said.

You are quite different from your things. You can own shelves of the classics of literature, bound in the finest leather, but be illiterate. You can cover your walls with expensive art, but have no love of beauty. You can own acres of land, but be narrow-minded. What you have has nothing to do with who you are.

{ .. .. }

If who you are is a God-graced person, the defining characteristic of your life is giving, not getting. You've already received the most important treasure in the universe: God loves you and has determined to be *for you* for all eternity. "Blessed be the God and Father of our Lord Jesus Christ," Paul wrote to the Ephesians, "who has blessed us in Christ with every spiritual blessing in the heavenly places, just as he chose us in Christ before the foundation of the world to be holy and blameless before him in love. He destined us for adoption as his children through Jesus Christ, according to the good pleasure of his will, to the praise of his glorious grace that he freely bestowed on us in the Beloved."[4] Even before the ink on the blueprints for the universe was dry, God chose you to be part of the family. In an exuberance of grace, God decided that you'd be home free before you were born, that you'd be found before you had a chance to get lost; this means you already have "every spiritual blessing in the heavenly places," which means there isn't a single bright, shining angel that has anything better than you have. There is no harp-strumming, bliss-bearing, joy-filled resident of heaven that's got anything more than *is already yours.*

Unless you've done the inane thing of rejecting this gift, you've already received more treasure than you'll ever accumulate by building bigger and bigger barns. Because you don't need to waste an ounce of energy grasping for stuff you don't need and can't keep, you have the freedom to join the dance and move with the rhythm of God's beating heart.

Karl Menninger, the famous psychiatrist, was once asked what he would advise a person who felt a nervous breakdown coming on; he said, "Lock up your house, go across the railway tracks, find someone in need and do something to help that person."[5] Psychological health, he seemed to be saying, could be found in the act of giving. Well, of course. God is the Prodigal Lover, the One who gives and gives and *never quits giving*—and therefore, as we give, we transcend our sick self-centeredness and become more Godlike.

In his spiritual memoir, *Returning,* Dan Wakefield tells of his experiences with years of psychoanalysis, the result of which left him in a deep, dark pit: "I had gone into psychoanalysis to save myself, and at about the same time I went to East Harlem in the hope of helping others. Looking back from the vantage point of thirty years it seems quite clear in a literal way that what I did to save myself nearly killed me . . . and what I did in the hope of helping others nourished and sustained me and maybe even saved my life."[6]

During my years as a pastor of two congregations and a president of a seminary, I got to know many people, and I made this observation: givers are happy people. I've known people who made me blush with embarrassment over my stinginess, and to a person their generosity elevated them to a higher level of joy. Not that they didn't experience the usual run of human problems; they had their own down days. But in general they were proof that it pays to be generous.

I once visited a Presbyterian medical clinic in Ghana, a long Land Rover ride away from my comfort zone. I was excited about my adventure, until they told me they had just killed a black mamba (one of the deadliest snakes in the world) right outside the door of the house I would be using. I mention this only to illustrate that those who lived at Donkorkrom Hospital had to put up with difficulties most of us can't imagine. Despite this, the happiness I witnessed surprised me. No one seemed to be "sacrificing," although that's exactly what they were doing. They appeared to be having a lot of fun.

The chief physician was Dr. Tim Hannah, an Australian who had left a successful medical practice in Europe. I said to him, "This is quite a change."

He replied, "Yes. I was making bundles of money, driving a new Porsche, and enjoying the comforts of affluence. But frankly, it was boring compared to this." Then, with a big smile on his face, he said, "This is really living!"

One day Tim took me out to a big field and announced it was time for a little recreation. Out of a bag he pulled a boomerang. "I'm from Australia, you know, and now I'm going to show you how to use one of these things." He was a good teacher; before long I was heaving that wooden wedge as hard as I could, and it was coming back to me. I can't begin to describe the physics of boomerang flight. All I know is, when I threw it hard away from me, it came flying back.[7]

Which is what Tim and other givers experience. It's the central paradox that Jesus taught: the ones who seek to save their lives will lose them, and the ones who sacrifice them will save them. Hoard what you have, and it will turn to dust in your hands; give it away, and you will gain far more than you lose.

{ .. .. }

Jesus said, "Give, and it will be given you. A good measure, pressed down, shaken together, running over, will be put into your lap; for the measure you give will be the measure you get back."[8]

The phrase "into your lap" probably refers to the large pocket in Middle Eastern clothing that was created by the belt and the fold in the robe just above the belt. Even this huge pocket won't be enough to hold the blessings pressed down, shaken together, and running over.

Can you picture it? A grain merchant fills his measuring container, while the customer looks at him in a way that says, "Come on, you can get more in there." He shakes it down. "I knew your mother, God rest her soul, and she didn't train you to be this stingy." Then he presses it down. "I took care of you when you were a baby, even changed your diapers, and this is how you show gratitude?" So with a defeated scowl he pours the grain until it's running over, falling all over the place.

This is the sort of overflowing abundance you can expect, Jesus said, if you give with a generous measure.

For many years, this text troubled me. I was never sure how to square it with the rest of the Gospel story. It seemed so antithetical to grace. Does God wait to see how much we give before giving to us? This would contradict the central New Testament teaching that God always gives more than we deserve, that we are the recipients of not only overflowing but *undeserved* abundance. Was Jesus so fully human that he sometimes had an off day?

I was confused, so I did what we usually do with a difficult-to-understand text: I ignored it. But one day I came across a paragraph in a remarkable essay by C. S. Lewis, and a light of understanding switched on:

> We must not be troubled by unbelievers when they say that this promise of reward makes the Christian life a mercenary affair. There are different kinds of rewards. There is a reward which has no natural connection with the things you do to earn it and is quite foreign to the desires that ought to accompany those things. Money is not the natural reward for love; that is why we call a man mercenary if he marries a woman for the sake of her money. But marriage is the proper reward for a real lover, and he is not mercenary for desiring it. A general who fights well in order to get a peerage is mercenary; a general who fights for victory is not, victory being the proper reward of battle as marriage is the proper reward for love. The proper rewards are not simply tacked on to the activity for which they are given, but are the activity itself in consummation.[9]

The activity itself in consummation. What is the reward for giving? The consummation of giving—pure giving, perfect giving. In other words, God. God is the One who "so loved the world that he *gave* his only Son." Every act of giving moves us closer to this source of primal generosity. The reward for giving is nothing less than God, a good measure pressed down and shaken together and running over.

Chapter Sixteen

Therefore Be Human

AS A CONCLUSION to this part of the book, we come to another welcome *therefore:* if the grace of God assures us that we've been set free from condemnation and destined for life (through our death), and if we can affirm the truth about ourselves with no equivocation or evasion, then we may relax in our humanity.

This is quite different from our usual *modus operandi.* Our sin, as we've seen, has made us want to take God's place, and our fear of death has fueled this desire. We have organized our lives and expended our energy attempting to gain control of our world. We have not been successful, of course, but this failure, far from discouraging us, has made us work all the harder to attain the impossible.

But then God did the impossible: God became like us. This was the great reversal that put us in our place and enabled us to stay there. Yes, we're broken and destined for death, but through Jesus Christ God healed us and guaranteed our life. No longer do we need to become like God; now we can be content with who we are.

Annie Dillard writes about our fumbling attempts at public worship: "A high school stage play is more polished than this service we have been rehearsing since the year one. In two thousand years, we have not worked out the kinks. . . . Week after week Christ washes the disciples' dirty feet, handles their very toes, and repeats, It is all right—believe it or not—to be people."[1]

It is all right to be people. Just people.

In Nikos Kazantzakis's novel *Christ Recrucified,* four village men are confessing their sins to one another in the presence of a "pope" (the Greek term for pastor):

> The pope seemed to guess their thoughts.
>
> "My children," he said, "an eye is open in us day and night, and watches. An ear is open deep in our heart, and listens: God."
>
> And Michelis cried:
>
> "How can God let us live on the earth? Why doesn't He kill us to purify creation?"
>
> "Because, Michelis," the pope answered, "God is a potter; He works in mud."[2]

God does not ask us to become gold or silver or a precious gem; God happily works with mud. What can be done with that? Well, do you know how Venice came to be built? Invading armies drove the inhabitants out of the area onto mud flats. With nowhere else to live, they dug canals and built bridges, and on top of mud they built a fabulous city. Now, if creatures who are nothing but mud themselves can build a Venice on mud, what might God do with this most humble element of the earth?

{ .. .. }

I don't have much problem believing this in a general sense—that is, God accepts humanity as a whole—but I have difficulty imagining how it could be true for me personally. Within my own skin, I'm too aware of my own inclinations and limitations, and it takes a tremendous leap of faith to think that *I* am acceptable.

Yet that is precisely what I may and must believe.

Many centuries ago a famous rabbi named Zuschia said, "On Judgment Day, God will not say to me, 'Zuschia, why were you not Moses?' God will say to me, 'Zuschia, why were you not Zuschia?' "[3]

God expects me to be myself, wanting nothing less than my strengths and nothing more than my weaknesses; if that appears too little, I must remember that God works in mud.

{ .. .. }

We would do well to ponder Jesus' last words on the cross: "It is finished."[4] In the Greek text, this is one word: *tetelestai*. It does not mean, "It is all over," or "It has come to an end," but rather "It is accomplished." Jesus was saying, "Everything is now completed, fulfilled."

Who can say this at the end of a single day, let alone at the close of a life? There always seems to be so much more to do, so little time to get it done.

In reflective moments, when we're doing our best to be objective, we can acknowledge that we're only human and that one person can't do everything. The problem, however, is a frequent short in the circuit between mind and guts. At an emotional level we often feel frustrated, even guilty, because we really do expect to *be* all things, in order to *do* all things, in order to *meet all expectations.*

Why? I'm not sure, but I suppose there are at least two reasons for most of us—one negative and one positive. Part of the problem, no doubt, is our lingering difficulty with pride. We haven't completely forsaken the desire to be in God's place. We like being at the center of things, with others dependent on us; we like being needed; we like being gods in our little world. There's also a positive motive in the mix: we want to make a difference for the better; we want to serve; we want to fulfill our personal potential. Consequently, we're running in a hundred directions, simultaneously feeling unfulfilled and worn out.

What human being has ever been able to say, "It is finished"? Alexander the Great conquered Persia, but he broke down and wept when it became evident that his troops were too exhausted to push on to India. Hugo Grotius, considered the father of modern international law, said at the last, "I have accomplished nothing worthwhile in my life." John Quincy Adams, president of the United States from 1825 to 1829—not a Lincoln, perhaps, but a good leader—wrote in his diary, "My life has been spent in vain and idle aspirations, and in ceaseless rejected prayers that something would be the result of my existence beneficial to my species." Robert Louis Stevenson wrote words that continue to delight and enrich our lives, yet what did he write for his epitaph? "Here lies one who meant well, who tried a little, and failed much." Cecil Rhodes opened up Africa and established an empire, but what were his dying words? "So little done, so much to do." Sir Francis Chichester, after fulfilling his life's dream by sailing around the world twice as fast as any other person, wrote that after his accomplishment he felt nothing but deep depression.[5]

But here is Jesus: "It is finished." John doesn't describe his tone of voice, though Matthew, Mark, and Luke say he died with a loud cry. This must be it. Not the resigned sigh of a defeated man, but the cry of victory. "It is accomplished!"

What, exactly, was accomplished? He was but a young man with many years of ministry ahead of him. He had been preaching only three years and had little to show for it: the last of his followers had beaten a hasty retreat; the kingdom of Rome was hardly threatened by the Kingdom of God; recovery of sight hadn't yet come to many who were still stumbling around in blindness; release to the captives might have been proclaimed, but more than a few were still doing time up the river; and liberty hadn't yet come to everyone living on the underside of society. In his final moments, he who had promised rivers of living water cried, "I thirst." He who had said, "My Father and I are one" cried out, "My God, my God, why have you forsaken me?" He who had said, "I am the resurrection and the life" was now dying.

So again, what was accomplished? Just this: what God had given him to do. The night before he died, Jesus prayed, "I glorified you on earth by finishing the work that you gave me to do."[6] Jesus did all that God asked him to do—and no more. How tempting it must have been for him to try to save the world. He had barely begun, after all. A few more years, and who could tell what might happen? Thousands more could hear his message of the Kingdom; at least hundreds more could be touched by its power—healed and set free from various kinds of oppression.

To the end, though, Jesus remained obedient to the Father who had sent him. He renounced many opportunities for influence in order to make one supreme sacrifice; he turned his back on efforts to save the world in favor of single-minded devotion to God—*and for that reason* he *did* save the world. Therein lies the paradox: Jesus emptied himself of even his exalted office of "savior" and his power to make a difference in the world, and through that self-limitation came his true glory as Reconciler. An act of intensive obedience became the extensive hope for the cosmos; at a point in time, just outside the gates of Jerusalem, Jesus did the one thing needful, and the effects are now eternal and universal.

{ .. .. }

If God did not consider our life, limited by time and space, to be too constricting, and if God moreover has embraced our particular life, limited by sin, we can relax and be content with being only human.

Yes, God has saved the whole of us and therefore has a claim on every part of us. As we shall see in the next part, we have been called to witness to the grace that has turned the world upside down. All that we are has been conscripted into this task. But only that. When we grasp at more, when we blush with embarrassment at modest gifts or limited opportunities, when we feverishly take on more responsibilities to prove how capable we are or how necessary, we are allowing pride to have its pernicious way in our lives. We would do well to remember that we're only mud, which is more than enough for God.

"It is finished." We, too, can say these words at the end of the day, and even at the end of our lives. We will not make everyone happy, but our only obligation is to make God happy. We will not be perfectly successful, but we're called only to be faithful. We will not accomplish all that could be done, but we're not responsible for that anyway. We will not be the savior of the world, not even our own little world, but thank God, Jesus already is.

Part Four

Upside-Down World

Chapter Seventeen

Love, Not Self-Centeredness

WHAT IS OUR purpose? We are loved by God, free to be human. But what is the point of our lives?

It might be hard to remember. Virginia Stem Owens describes how easy it is to get distracted:

> The spy slowly begins to forget his mission. He spends so much time and effort learning the language, adopting the habits and customs, internalizing the thought patterns flawlessly, that somehow, gradually, imperceptibly, he becomes his cover. He forgets what he's about. He goes to school, grows up. He gets a job, collects his pay, buys a house, waters the lawn. He settles down and settles in. He wakes up each morning with the shape of his mission, which brought him here in the first place, grown hazier, like a dream that slides quickly away. He frowns and makes an effort to remember. But the

> phone rings or the baby cries, and he is distracted for the rest of the day.[1]

Owens says our vocation is to be spies, in the sense that we have "a lifelong task of figuring out the world,"[2] and that we, like Shakespeare's Lear, should "take upon 's the mystery of things, / As if we were God's spies."[3] Our mission is to collect information, to make sense of the world.

Although that may be part of our job description, I suggest that we're called to be spies in the more radical, dubious sense of the term: undercover agents sent to subvert the present order. In the current regime, ego sits on the throne, as individuals and institutions selfishly accumulate influence, power, and control. But in the new regime, inaugurated in Jesus Christ, self-giving is the way of life. The realm of God, as Jesus proclaimed it, is the reign of love. We ourselves have been claimed by that love, and now we're appointed agents of it. Grace receivers are to become grace dispensers; the loved are to become lovers.

Jesus said, " 'You shall love the Lord your God with all your heart, and with all your soul, and with all your mind.' This is the greatest and first commandment. And a second is like it: 'You shall love your neighbor as yourself.' On these two commandments hang all the law and prophets."[4] Then, during his last meal with his disciples, he summarized the essence of his teaching, the point of everything he had been trying to say and do: "I give you a new commandment, that you love one another. Just as I have loved you, you also should love one another. By this everyone will know that you are my disciples, if you have love for one another."[5]

⁂{ .. .. }⁂

Few words in English are more used or abused than *love.* We apply it to everything from eggplant Parmesan to warm weather, and from the affections of parents to the attractions of sex. No wonder Aldous Huxley wrote that "of all the worn, smudged, dog's-eared words in our vocabulary, *love* is surely the grubbiest, smelliest, slimiest. Bawled from a million pulpits, lasciviously crooned through hundreds of millions of loudspeakers, it has become an outrage to good taste and decent feeling, an obscenity which one hesitates to pronounce. And yet, it has to be pronounced, for, after all, love is the last word."

What did Jesus mean when he commanded his followers to love one another? The Greek text employs the word *agape,* which was little used until the New Testament writers adopted it and filled it with meaning. It describes not a feeling or an emotion but an action; it refers not to romantic attraction *(eros)* or to friendship *(philos)* but to self-giving. We learn the meaning of this word from God's love for us. More than a sentiment, God's love is the supreme self-sacrifice that affirms, forgives, upholds, and grants life; it heals and builds up, renews and resurrects.

"What does it mean to love one's neighbor?" Karl Barth asks. "It means to stand surety for him, to make ourselves responsible for him, to offer and give ourselves to him. . . . It consists in the fact that (whether he likes him and can earn his liking or not) the one interposes himself for the other, making himself his guarantor and desire nothing else but to be this. . . . He delivers himself to this other with the sole purpose of guaranteeing in his own person the fact that God loves him too, and that he too is free to love God."[6]

Jesus embodied this love in the world, and if we follow him—if we are Christians—our mission is to do the same. But the cross atop Golgotha should give us pause. The world doesn't take kindly to subversion. It may not crucify us, as it did Jesus, but the world will do its best to squeeze us into a mold, exert every possible pressure to keep us operating out of our own self-interest. "If you don't look out for yourself, no one else will," the world tells us. Be good to yourself, believe in yourself, take care of yourself, protect yourself, pamper yourself, reward yourself, baby yourself, love yourself—look out for numero uno! We internalize these thought patterns flawlessly, becoming our cover. We settle down and settle in.

As if the cultural pressures aren't enough, we've got more than a few internal ones besides. To a large extent, our lives are still structured by sin, which is to say we are still oriented, first and foremost, toward ourselves. We want what the culture tells us we deserve.

So we have a major problem. How can we turn outward toward God and the world in love, when a centripetal force constantly pulls us inward? How can we fulfill our mission?

We can't. We do not have the power to become lovers. We have neither the inclination nor the character to give ourselves to the needs of others, let alone sacrifice ourselves. To be sure, every now and then we hear stories of heroic sacrifice, such as the firefighters on September 11 racing up the towers of the World Trade Center before they collapsed, and we like to imagine that we too would be as courageous. Perhaps we would, in extraordinary circumstances. But what happens in ordinary circumstances? What about a steady offering of ourselves to the needs of others—family members, certainly, but also neighbors, obnoxious coworkers, the worn woman holding a placard at the exit ramp, those who have hurt us, and all the burned-out and beat-up we come across? That's another matter, isn't it?

We'd have to be Christ to love like that.

That's why God is transforming us into the image of Christ.

{ .. .. }

This transformation is the work of the Holy Spirit, the third person of the trinity. God is the triunity of the Father who sends the Son, the Son who obeys the Father, and the Spirit who binds them together in love. Imagine the love between the Father and the Son as being so perfect, so intimate, so personal, that it is itself a third Person. God is the fellowship of these three persons, and part of the never-ending work of divine grace is the sharing of this love with us. The same Spirit that dwells within the Father and the Son is present in our lives, guiding us and working within us; the Holy Spirit is God's power transforming us into the image of Christ. The Apostle Paul said that "all of us . . . seeing the glory of the Lord as though reflected in a mirror, are being transformed into the same image from one degree of glory to another; for this comes from the Lord, the Spirit."[7]

The indwelling of the Holy Spirit doesn't happen all at once, contrary to what some say. To be sure, you might get zapped and speak in tongues, or see a vision, or fall flat in ecstatic wonder (these things sometimes happen), but however powerfully you've been "slain in the Spirit" you must sooner or later get back to ordinary life, which often includes loving people you don't even like. There comes a time, in other words, when you have to turn out the lights in the sanctuary and go home, and on the way home you'll still be enough of the same person you were before that you might get angry with your spouse, or yell at the jerk who cut you off on the freeway, or start brooding about the next day when you'll have to face that miserable back-stabber at the office.

For reasons known only to God (and lamented by me), the Holy Spirit doesn't seem to be in any hurry with this project of making us more loving. The transformation seems to proceed at a pace only slightly faster than a glacier, and sometimes it even seems to reverse itself. If you charted the average person's change toward Christlikeness, it would not be a straight-line trajectory. When my daughter was a little girl, she decided to celebrate St. Patrick's Day by dipping the feet of her pet hamster in green paint (she wanted to fool the family into thinking a leprechaun had visited), and I can still see the trail of footprints, backward and forward, zigzagging all over the place. That's about what a map of our spiritual journey looks like. Most days, we don't seem to be getting anywhere at all; we still struggle with the self-centeredness, we still hurt others, and we still disappoint ourselves.

But—here's the Gospel truth—we're making progress, believe it or not. Jesus promises his Spirit to those who follow him, and when we open ourselves to the Spirit's influence new attributes grow within us. "The fruit of the Spirit," Paul wrote, "is love, joy, peace, patience, kindness, generosity, faithfulness, gentleness, and self-control"[8]—a perfect description of the life of Jesus Christ.

{ .. .. }

The Holy Spirit turns us inside out, enabling us to move from self-centeredness to self-sacrifice, to turn from our own concerns to those of the world around us. The Holy Spirit, in other words, continues the work of God's grace, causing the love that was outside us (claiming us) to become a love that is inside us (empowering us).

This power was at work in my friend Frank, who was, before he retired, a hard-driving corporate attorney, a can-do personality who did everything with a take-no-prisoners fervor. A few years ago, he wanted to give himself more fully to someone in need, so he picked Steve, a young Marine captain dying of ALS (Lou Gehrig's disease). Frank cared for him until the paralysis squeezed the last breath out of Steve. After Steve's death, Frank moved on to Howard, who had been diagnosed with cancer. He stuck with Howard too, holding his hand until the day it grew limp and cold. Then, with Howard dispatched to the Lord's eternal embrace, Frank turned his energies toward Bill, a well-known physician in his late fifties who had just been diagnosed with Alzheimer's disease. "This is going to be tough," Frank told me, "but I've signed on for the long haul." He stayed with Bill and his family through the long season of suffering. He even flew with Bill to Arizona to watch the San Diego Padres in spring training. When they returned, he said, "Don, we sure had some *interesting* experiences, but it was great! I took my son with us, because I wanted to show him that this is just what disciples of Jesus do, that we're to love one another."

Yes, disciples love one another. This love, though, is not exclusive, reserved only for those in the family of faith. It flows from the love of God, after all, and that's a love for the whole world.

Richard Selzer, a surgeon with an extraordinary gift of writing, describes a memorable scene:

> I stand by the bed where a young woman lies, her face postoperative, her mouth twisted in palsy, clownish. A tiny twig of the facial nerve, the one to the muscles of her mouth, has been severed. She will be thus from now on. The surgeon had followed with religious fervor the curve of her flesh; I promise you that. Nevertheless, to remove the tumor in her cheek, I had to cut the little nerve.
>
> Her young husband is in the room. He stands on the opposite side of the bed, and together they seem to dwell in the evening lamplight, isolated from me, private. Who are they, I ask myself, he and this wry-mouth I have made, who gaze at and touch each other so generously, greedily? The young woman speaks.
>
> "Will my mouth always be like this?" she asks.
>
> "Yes," I say, "it will. It is because the nerve was cut."

> She nods and is silent. But the young man smiles.
>
> "I like it," he says. "It is kind of cute."
>
> All at once I *know* who he is. I understand, and I lower my gaze. One is not bold in an encounter with a god. Unmindful, he bends to kiss her crooked mouth, and I am so close I can see how he twists his own lips to accommodate to hers, to show her that their kiss still works.[9]

Disciples of Jesus twist their lips to accommodate the world's crooked, needy mouth. The remaining chapters of this book attempt to describe the shape of this kiss.

Love, Not Self-Centeredness

Chapter Eighteen

Affirmation, Not Condemnation

IN A CONGREGATION I once served, an older man would occasionally shake my hand following a worship service and say, in a grim voice, "Today, you weren't preaching. You were meddling."

You might think I've stopped preaching and started meddling here, for we are now considering how grace turns upside down our relationship with other people—people, let's admit it, who at their best can be annoying and at their worst disgusting. We've already seen how grace causes an upheaval in our relationship with God and ourselves; however disconcerting, this turns out to be good news. So why don't we quit while we're ahead? Why don't we just take the offering, have a closing prayer, and get on with the rest of our lives?

Well, that's precisely the problem. Grace does want us to get on with the rest of our lives, which, as it turns out, includes other people. The grace that has freely and completely embraced us, the grace that has enabled us to stand with dignity and delight—this very grace works for others too.

Paul's letter to Christians in Rome is a long treatise that says, in short, everyone has sinned but everyone has been saved. He stresses the *everyone* in both instances because humanity shares an essential solidarity. We're children of Adam, and his disobedience has broken us all. But we're also brothers and sisters of Jesus Christ, and his obedience has healed us all. "For if many died through the one man's trespass, much more surely have the grace of God and the free gift in the grace of the one man, Jesus Christ."

The apostle is struggling to communicate a complicated truth here, and it seems he has second thoughts about the way he's expressing it before the ink dries on the parchment, even before he finishes the sentence. He doesn't want to imply that sin and death are equal to grace and life. So he says, "If many have died . . ." *Many?* Do you know anyone who hasn't died or isn't about to die? But he uses *many* to set up a contrast with the next phrase, where he uses "much more." Odd as it sounds, the effects of sin are total, but grace is more than total; though death claims everyone, life claims more than everyone. Clearly, he's gotten himself into a situation every writer can identify with: his words aren't big enough to hold the truth, but rather than retreat and regroup he turns up the volume, picks up the pace, and refuses to let go until they make his point: "If, because of the one man's trespass, death exercised dominion through that one, much more surely will those who receive the abundance of grace and the free gift of righteousness exercise dominion in life through the one man, Jesus Christ. Therefore, just as one man's trespass led to condemnation for all, so one man's act of righteousness leads to justification and life for all."[1] The controlling part of the sentence is "much more." Grace pushes language beyond logic; it is always *much more.*

Most especially, it is much more extensive and far broader than we're ready to acknowledge. Through Jesus Christ, God freely, unreservedly, indiscriminately, and without quibbling or qualifying reaches out and embraces everyone. That includes you and me, for sure, but also your Aunt Agnes, wino Wiley curled up in the stairwell of a flophouse, and even Osama bin Laden and Saddam Hussein.

Yes, grace is this inclusive. It may be true that all these people, including your Aunt Agnes, are fleeing God's grace, but then, as we've discovered, this hardly distinguishes them from us. Haven't we too in our own way resisted the Mercy? Nowhere do we put up a stiffer fight than right here at this point: God may love sinners in general, but who wants to believe that God is *for* an Osama bin Laden or Saddam Hussein in particular?

Grace calls us not only to believe this but to join in the embrace. Since we ourselves have been saved by grace, we are now grace-claimed, conscripted into the service of grace, called to become grace-filled and grace-directed. We ourselves have been swept up by the river of God's affirmation, and now we are asked to stay in the current that's flowing toward others.

{ .. .. }

Do I hear a whistle blowing? You say we need a time-out? Fine, let's deal with your objections.

You think I'm taking things too far? You think that Aunt Agnes, however much she tries to run your life by passing on the latest advice from Dr. Laura, is obviously a much better person than Osama bin Laden or Saddam Hussein? That if what I say is true, grace is an unfair equalizer?

I have three things to say. First, I have nothing against your aunt. I am sure that neither the terrorist nor the dictator are worthy to lick the mud off her black pumps. It might be worth noting, however, that buried within the heart of each of them may be the same desire to control others, even if the means and opportunity of expressing it vary enormously. But I won't press the issue.

Second, let me remind you of our situation. We're living in an interim time. Because of universal self-centeredness, life is a mess—for us and for everyone else. Genuine evil is afoot. For now, then, we have no choice but to make distinctions between good and bad. We must try to discern the right and try to do it, neither of which is easy given our limited knowledge and crooked hearts. But we cannot evade the responsibility.

Still, if we are following Jesus, albeit with half-hearted resolve and constant stumbling, we are citizens in good standing of another realm, a realm where grace rules. Though it has not yet arrived in fullness, it's on the way, and we are called to be people of this future. Therefore—let me repeat: *therefore*—all judgments we make must be motivated by grace and aim toward fulfillment of grace. We may indeed need to tell our children that some behavior is wrong. We may need to confront a friend about his drug addiction. We may need to take to the streets in protest of some laws. We may need to send criminals to jail. We may even need to send the Marines into Afghanistan and Iraq. We may need to make ethical distinctions and act upon them in this broken world. But we cannot endorse anything unless it ultimately, and perhaps in a way we only vaguely apprehend, serves the purposes of grace, which is to say unless it aims not for revenge but for reconciliation, not for destruction but for restoration, not for death but for life, not for condemnation but for salvation.

Third, you're right: grace is an unfair equalizer. *Nolo contendere.*

⁂

Grace for everyone is as difficult to swallow as liver because we're more comfortable in a world of good guys and bad guys, where we can designate who's in and who's out; this is the world that has shaped us, after all, the one we consider normal. Frankly, given even half a warrant, we actually like to condemn others. Something within us, largely unconscious, finds no little pleasure in putting people down, if not as far as hell then certainly well below us.

You'll be happy to hear there are reasons for this, some of which are illuminated by psychology. Carl Jung taught that every individual has a persona and a shadow. The persona (the name given to the masks worn by ancient actors to signify roles they played) is the part of ourselves we present to the public. It's oriented toward society, and it helps us adapt to the expectations of others. It enables us to define ourselves according to the circumstances, as we assume the masks of parent, lover, student, friend, professional, and so on. The persona is a necessary accoutrement of social life.

The shadow, on the other hand, is the darker side of our personality, which we don't consciously display in public and don't even display to ourselves. In the words of psychotherapist June Singer:

> It is what is inferior in our personality, that part of us which we will not allow ourselves to express. The stronger and more rigid the persona, and the more we identify with it, the more we must deny the other important aspects of our personality. These aspects are repressed to the unconscious, and they contribute to the formation of a more or less autonomous splinter-personality, the shadow. The shadow finds its own means of expression, though, particularly through projection. What we cannot admit in ourselves we often find in others. If, when an individual speaks of another person whom he hates with a vehemence that seems nearly irrational, he can be brought to describe that person's characteristics which he most dislikes, you will frequently have a picture of his own repressed aspects, which are unrecognized by him though obvious to others. The shadow is a dominant of the personal unconscious and consists of all those uncivilized desires and emotions that are incompatible with the social standards and with the persona; it is all that we are ashamed of.[2]

Affirmation, Not Condemnation

The shadow, by definition, prefers the dark. Dragging unpleasant parts of our personality into the light is not easy. Not only do we dislike learning unpleasant things about ourselves, we especially dislike losing the illusion that we're in control of our lives. So we identify with our persona, trying to convince ourselves and everyone else that this is who we really are, and we keep our shadow buried in the cellar beneath our awareness.

But the shadow always escapes, one way or another. Dark things we deny about ourselves eventually come out, often through our projections. When we're upset with others, we're very likely casting on them parts of our own shadow. When the Pharisee in Jesus' parable said, "God, I thank you that I am not like other people: thieves, rogues, adulterers, or even like this tax collector," you can assume that all these sinners were alive and well and kicking up the dust of his own unconscious fears and obsessions.

Kirk Fordice, as governor of Mississippi, made himself a symbol of family values. When President Clinton's affair with Monica Lewinsky became public, Fordice was a fierce critic and called for his resignation. Then Fordice's own long-running extramarital affair was exposed. According to syndicated columnist Cynthia Tucker, "The latest twist in Mississippi's favorite soap opera came . . . with a flurry of news reports that Fordice had vacationed in France with a woman to whom he was not married. The revelation forced him to announce that he will divorce his wife of 44 years and marry Memphis widow Ann Creson, his junior-high sweetheart, with whom he had been linked over the years."[3]

I don't mean to single out the governor as extraordinary. We all have things we'd prefer not to be made public. My point is simply that when we make judgments against others, we may be endeavoring to keep something hidden in ourselves.

I would like to believe that my condemnation of a friend's materialism, or a preacher's arrogance, or a politician's ambition—things that push my emotional buttons—are based on an objective assessment of the situation, on clear-thinking evaluation. But truth to tell, they more often reflect my own struggles with these things, which I try to keep out of sight by deflecting attention toward others.

{ .. .. }

"Do not judge," Jesus said. He said it again and again, in sermons and parables and by his own personal example. Jesus was the embodiment of grace, as we've seen, but he frequently delivered severe judgments against those who were judgmental. He got along famously with almost everyone—prostitutes and corrupt IRS officials, party-hardies and wheeler-dealers and experienced swingers—but the people he couldn't tolerate and constantly rebuked were those who thought they were righteous, who looked down their straight and narrow noses at others. "Why do you see the speck in your neighbor's eye, but do not notice the log in your own eye?"[4]

We don't see the log in our own eye because we don't want to see it, because we've buried it in the shadows. So we keep ourselves busy pointing out specks in the eyes of others.

Affirmation, Not Condemnation

Here's the good news: Jesus' stern warning against judging others is itself part of God's grace; this prohibition is a signpost to freedom. Do not judge, because you don't have to! Remember, you have been accepted by God, wholly and unconditionally. Grace has claimed you, and this grace enables you to be honest about yourself, even the darkest and most secret aspects of your own life. Therefore you do not need to hide behind your precious persona and project onto others your fearful shadow.

Do not judge, moreover, because it doesn't work. It can only tear down, not build up. If you want be in step with the rhythm of the universe, if you want to be a person of grace, if you *truly* want to love others and want to help them become all they were created to be, you will not condemn, because *condemnation never saves anyone.*

When I am condemned, a part of me always rises up in self-defense. The instinct for self-preservation is so basic it will not allow me *not* to defend myself when threatened. So if you take it upon yourself to hammer me with righteous judgments about my failures (which may be considerable), I will not suddenly feel sorry for what I've done and repent in humility. I will do just the opposite: I will identify even more completely with my persona, and I will push my failure even further into the shadows.

Condemnation can only inflict more pain. It is useful, I suppose, in venting anger and meting out vengeance. But it cannot lift the fallen or restore the broken. It might make the person who uses it feel superior and it might hide insecurities; it might help polish the persona and it might keep the shadow in the cellar. But it will never save.

This should be obvious when we consider how God chose to deal with the failures of this world: "For God so loved the world that he gave his only Son, so that everyone who believes in him may not perish but have eternal life. Indeed, God did not send the Son into the world to condemn the world, but in order that the world might be saved through him."[5] God saved the world through love, not condemnation; God restored broken creation through grace, not judgment. The Devil, remember, is the one whom Scripture calls the Accuser. God is the Affirmer.

Grace alone has the power to change people for the better. Only in the capacious freedom of having already been accepted can people own their failures and walk down another path. Grace alone grants the courage to face wrongdoing; grace alone grants the ability to keep things in perspective, to see failure as only one thread in the larger tapestry of life; grace alone grants the strength to rise up with confidence to face a new future.

{ .. .. }

During a difficult season of my life, when parts of my shadow were emerging into the light of consciousness, a wise therapist told me about a friend of hers who discovered, while doing research in South Africa, an unusual way of administering justice. In the Bambemba tribe, a person who has acted irresponsibly or done something wrong is placed in the center of the village, alone and unfettered. All work ceases, and all the men, women, and children gather in a larger circle around the accused. Then each person, one by one, speaks to him about all the good things he has done in his lifetime. Yes, the *good* things. Every incident and every experience that can be recalled is recounted as accurately as possible. All positive attributes, generous deeds, strengths, and kindnesses are recited carefully and at length. No one is permitted to fabricate or exaggerate or be facetious. This ceremony often lasts several days and does not cease until everyone is drained of every positive comment that can be made about the person in question. Then the circle is broken, a joyous celebration takes place, and the person is welcomed back into the tribe.[6]

I know nothing about the Bambemba tribe, but I can tell you this: they are not far from what Jesus called the Kingdom of God.

Chapter Nineteen

Forgiving, Not Keeping Score

ONE SUNDAY, AS a young pastor, I was leading my congregation in the Lord's Prayer. For some reason, I skipped over the phrase "forgive us our debts as we forgive our debtors." I went straight from "give us this day our daily bread" to "lead us not into temptation." As I blasted this boo-boo through the microphone, I heard stifled snickers through the sanctuary. I botched something any Sunday School child knows, and I've since wondered if my mistake signaled an unconscious discomfort with this part of the prayer. I'm willing and eager to pray for my own forgiveness, to be sure, but linking it to my forgiveness of others is unsettling.

If you've visited a number of churches, you know there is some disagreement about the translation of this petition. Presbyterians have debts, Episcopalians have trespasses, and others have sins. The word we use doesn't much matter, although I think *debts* more accurately translates Matthew's version of this prayer—a word that reflects the rabbinical idea that every sin creates a debt before God, the accumulation of which forms a wall of separation between us and God. Sins were thought of as demerits, and the corporate name for them was debts.[1]

It's wonderful to know these debts can be canceled. But forgive us our debts, *as we forgive our debtors?* What's this all about? Has the brightness of God's grace been dimmed by a cloud of conditional stipulation?

Commentators debate whether the second phrase should be seen as a condition or a consequence of God's forgiveness. Do we ask for forgiveness because we have forgiven, or do we forgive as a result of having been forgiven?

We must understand this petition in the context of the whole Gospel. The only condition for forgiveness is the perfect obedience of Jesus Christ. He took our place, as we have seen, doing for us what we could not do for ourselves—and that includes forgiving others on our behalf. He fulfilled *for us* the command to love our enemies; as he hung on the cross he prayed, "Father, forgive them,"[2] and because he was our representative, we have prayed that prayer in him. Having received this grace, then, how can we not continue the prayer and offer forgiveness to others? Because our debts have been canceled, how can we not readily cancel the debts of those who have wronged us? Forgive us our debts, we pray, *as of course we forgive others.*

{ .. .. }

Jesus' talk about forgiveness got Peter wondering about something: How much forgiveness should we offer to others? There are some people who never feel any remorse, who are incorrigible wrongdoers, who never appreciate the gift of a second chance. Surely, there must be limits. How many times should we forgive repeat offenders? I don't believe Peter was looking for loopholes; rather, he wanted to show Jesus that he was beginning to understand the importance of mercy, that he knew we should be *very* forgiving. "As many as seven times?" Peter asked. He must have felt pretty good about himself, making the wildly merciful guess of *seven times.* He must have thought the teacher would move him to the head of the class.

But Jesus dumbfounded him: "Nice try, Peter, but you're not even close. How about seventy times seven?" Then, seeing Peter's bewilderment, Jesus told another story to illustrate what it was like to live in God's realm.

A certain king wished to settle accounts with his slaves, one of whom owed ten thousand talents. In that day's currency one talent was worth more than fifteen years' wages, which in today's currency, by my calculation, comes to 123 gazillion dollars. Jesus didn't mention how a slave managed to accumulate such a debt, but it's safe to assume he must have had a few extremely bad nights at the poker table. He owed an absurd amount of money, more than he would ever be able to repay. So just as the king was ready to sell every inch of his unlucky hide, along with his wife and kids and all his possessions, the slave fell to his knees and rendered a performance worthy of an Academy Award. He begged for a little more time, promising to pay it all back. Right. How would a slave come up with 123 gazillion dollars? The king would be certifiably nuts to believe him, and of course he didn't.

But the king did something equally crazy: he took pity on him and forgave his debt. He tore up the slave's page in the ledger. Why would he do this? This was no way to run a kingdom; this would undermine the rule of law, thus destroying the foundation of the political order. The king must have gone through a kind of death. Robert Capon helped me see this: "He simply drops dead to the whole business of bookkeeping and forgives the servant."[3] This "death" allowed the debtor to live, and make no mistake about it, it upended everything, turned the world upside down.

The slave, as we have seen, was not too swift, and he clung to his folly with tenacity. On the way out of the palace, dancing down the wide marble steps and humming the "Ode to Joy," he met someone who owed him just a hundred denarii—about three months' wages—and demanded payment. When the poor fellow begged for time to pay him back, the slave had him thrown in prison. The one who had been forgiven 150,000 years of wages couldn't forgive three months' worth; the one who had received a mountain of mercy couldn't extend a thimbleful of it.

Word of this eventually reached the king, and he was none too happy. "Should you not have had mercy on your fellow slave, as I had mercy on you?" he asked. Then he gave orders to torture the ingrate until he paid the entire debt. If this story were a movie, you'd leave the theater grumbling, especially since you're left wondering how the poor wretch could earn a single denarius while being tortured and held in prison.

If that wasn't enough of a downer, Jesus concluded by saying, "So my heavenly Father will also do to every one of you, if you do not forgive your brother or sister from your heart."[4] You can either live in the old world, the world of law and consequences, or you can live in the upside down world, the world of grace. Take your pick. If you decide to stick with the familiar world you've always considered right side up, then you too will be treated that way, and it won't be much fun. You'll get the justice you demand, and it will begin with you.

⁂

In my first congregation, the one where I botched the Lord's Prayer, was a retired couple, Ray and Alma, who played a great deal of golf. One day Ray invited me to play a round with him, and I maintained my usual standard of excellence, whacking balls into every rough and sand trap. With frustration mounting to a near-violent level, I said, "You know, I'm wondering how you and Alma do this. Isn't it stressful on your marriage?"

Ray said, "Alma and I have learned the secret to enjoying golf. We never keep score."

That's the best way to get through the game of life too. In fact, it's the only way to play in a world turned upside down by grace. To forgive others means that we refuse to keep score, so the game can continue.

"Forgive and forget," the saying goes. It's nonsense. We do not need to forgive things we can forget; the annoyances that come from living around other people—there are usually plenty—don't require forgiveness, just the courtesy of ignoring them or not making a big deal of them. We're all dependent on this kindness; it's the lubrication that allows us to rub against each other without the social machinery breaking down. But we need to forgive precisely the things we can't forget: the meanness, the mockery, the betrayals, all the wrongs that have wounded us. If we've been deeply hurt, we'll likely be unable to forget it, at least not for a long time. Thus we need forgiveness to move forward into a future.

Forgiveness does not mean coming to a mutual understanding about what happened; sometimes people can't explain their own actions to themselves, let alone to anyone else. Besides, no two people will ever remember a past circumstance in exactly the same way. Nor does forgiveness mean that we no longer hurt, that our wounds have fully healed; some injuries keep throbbing with pain, which is why we can't forget them.

Forgiveness means that despite all this, we choose not to let bitterness destroy the relationship. We continue as a friend or spouse or colaborer without keeping score. The relationship may not be the same, especially if a serious wrong has been done. A spouse, for example, may forgive adultery, letting go of bitterness and offering goodwill to the guilty party, yet still conclude that the marriage has been irreparably broken. But despite not being able to forget, and the presence of pain, and changed circumstances, forgiveness means going forward in a way that, if possible, preserves the relationship, and if not then at least wishes the wrongdoer well. Obviously, forgiving an insensitive friend is different from forgiving a cheating spouse, but both instances require an act of will, a decision not to grant a wholly destructive power to the wrong.

"Forgiveness," Paul Tillich said, "means reconciliation in spite of estrangement; it means reunion in spite of hostility; it means acceptance of those who are unacceptable; and it means reception of those who are rejected."[5] The key words are *in spite of.*

❦ .. .. ❦

Charles Williams, writing during the blitz in London, said there are those things that need not be forgiven (where we have just misunderstood another person), those that need to be forgiven (ordinary actions of hurt and thoughtlessness, which we all commit), and those things that cannot be forgiven (the horrors of war and the systematic oppression and torture occurring all around the world)—and that the Christian needs to forgive them all.[6]

Surely, the atrocities committed at Ravensbruck concentration camp were among those things that cannot be forgiven. When Allied troops liberated the camp in 1945, they found an indescribable horror in which ninety-two thousand women and children had been killed. These words were found written on a piece of paper near the body of a dead child:

O Lord,
Remember not only the men and women of goodwill,
But also those of ill will.
But do not only remember the suffering they have
inflicted on us,
Remember the fruits we brought thanks to this suffering,
Our comradeship, our loyalty, our humanity,
The courage, the generosity,
The greatness of heart which has grown out of all this.
And when they come to judgement
Let all the fruits that we have borne
Be their forgiveness.[7]

How could anyone have such generosity? To ask forgiveness of one's enemies, even as they are killing one, requires an ability to rise above circumstance and pain, a transcendence of spirit that is Godlike, that comes from the Spirit of a forgiving God. This Spirit dwelt in Jesus, who, with his hands and feet nailed to a Roman cross, prayed, "Father, forgive them; for they do not know what they are doing." And this Spirit dwelt in Stephen, the first martyr of the Church, who, as he was being stoned to death, cried out, "Lord, do not hold this sin against them."[8]

As I sit in the comfort of my study, I wonder: Could I pray like this if my life were being taken from me? My imagination stumbles. I'm afraid my heart is too small, too easily clogged with anger and resentments. If I'm struck, I want to strike back. I do not know how to live in a world turned upside down, a world of grace that forgives those who do not deserve it. But I have received mercy myself, and God knows I want to pass it on.

My consolation is this: the spirit of forgiveness is the Spirit of God, the very same Holy Spirit promised to us as followers of Jesus. What we cannot do ourselves, the Holy Spirit enables to happen through us. So we continue to pray, perhaps with some trembling, "and forgive us our debts as we forgive our debtors."

{ .. .. }

Forgiveness is both an act and a gift of grace. When we forgive others, we extend grace; we *do* it. At the same time, we receive grace; we *enjoy* it. Forgiveness is first of all a blessing to the one who forgives; it makes possible release from bitterness and healing from injury. The South African writer Alan Paton said, "There is a hard law . . . that when a deep injury is done to us, we never recover until we forgive."[9]

Brennan Manning relates a story that Laurens Van der Post told about two brothers:

> The elder brother was strong, tall, intelligent, an excellent athlete. Sent away to a private school in South Africa where the family lived, he became an admired leader of the student body. His brother was some six years younger. Neither good-looking nor capable, he was also a hunchback. But he had one great gift. He had a magnificent singing voice. . . .
>
> Eventually the younger brother joined the older at the same boarding school. One day, in a cruel outbreak of mob psychology, a group of students ganged up on the younger brother, jeered at him, and tore off his shirt to reveal his hunchback.
>
> The older brother was aware of what was going on. He could have gone out and faced the crowd of

sadistic students, acknowledged the strange hunchback as his brother, and put a stop to the whole sorry mess. Instead he remained in the chemistry lab completing an assignment. He betrayed his brother by what he failed to do.

The younger brother was never the same again. He returned home to his parent's farm where he kept to himself and sang no more. Meanwhile the older brother had become a soldier in World War II, stationed in Palestine. One night, lying outdoors and gazing into the starlit sky, he realized what he had done to his younger brother in their school days. His heart told him that he would never have peace until he went home and asked his brother for forgiveness. And so he made the incredibly difficult wartime journey from Palestine to South Africa. The brothers talked long into the night, the elder one confessing his guilt and remorse. They cried together, embraced, and the breach between them was healed.

Something else happened that night. The older brother had fallen asleep when he was startled awake by the sound of a full, rich mellifluous voice soaring into the night. It was the beautiful voice of his younger brother who was singing once again.[10]

Forgiving others enables us to find a voice for singing. By choosing to live in God's upside-down world, we find ourselves moving with the flow of grace, and that means we are closer to the heart of God, a place of freedom and healing.

Chapter Twenty

Serving, Not Using

IN A WORLD turned upside down by grace, we serve people rather than use them.

The logic of this is plain: if God has embraced us, we have no need to use people to advance our own interests; if God has embraced other people too, we have every reason to use ourselves to advance their interests. After all, God is *for* them. To move with God is to move toward others in grace. The second great commandment, according to Jesus, is to love our neighbors as ourselves. This love—*agape*—has less to do with feelings than with actions; it means to stand surety for others, as we've seen, to offer ourselves for the benefit of those in need.

When Jesus headed for Jerusalem, his disciples knew it wasn't going to be a vacation. Mark's account says that "Jesus was walking ahead of them; they were amazed, and those who followed were afraid." Going to Jerusalem meant that Jesus was meeting head-on the religious and political authorities, that he was ready to precipitate the final clash between the reign of law and order and the reign of love and grace.

Neither the political nor the religious authorities would be happy about this. No wonder the disciples followed, at some distance I would guess, and with more than a little worry.

Jesus didn't mollify their fear. He warned that by going to Jerusalem he was as good as dead. He said, "We are going up to Jerusalem, and the Son of Man will be handed over to the chief priests and the scribes, and they will condemn him to death; then they will mock him, and spit upon him, and flog him, and kill him; and after three days he will rise again."[1]

At that point, had I been one of his followers, I would have remembered some business that needed my immediate attention up in Galilee, such as scrapping crud off my fishing boat or reroofing my mother-in-law's house—anything to keep me away from Jerusalem until the trouble blew over.

Instead, James and John sidled up to Jesus with a request. "Teacher, we want you to do for us whatever we ask of you." How's that for a way to begin? "Grant us to sit, one at your right hand and one at your left, in your glory."

Weren't they listening? Jesus had just said he was about to have the life tortured out of him, and they're worried about the seating arrangements in glory?

Either they hadn't heard Jesus or—I think this is more likely—they thought Jesus' prediction of his death and resurrection meant the revolution was beginning. God's Kingdom was about to be established, with Jesus sitting on the throne. So they wanted to push themselves to the head of the line before anyone else did; they wanted to be seated on the right and left of Jesus, in the next two highest positions of influence. Secretary of state, maybe, and secretary of defense, but no lousy ambassadorship to Ethiopia. After all, they had been with Jesus from the very beginning, and along with Peter were part of the disciples' inner circle. As for Peter . . . well, a first-class fisherman, certainly, but a little too (how shall we put it?) *mercurial,* not the sort of temperament for political leadership. All things considered, who better than the sons of Zebedee to be first and second deputies?

A request like this, you would think, should be made in private. Why didn't they pull Jesus aside and whisper their aspirations? Perhaps they felt secrecy was unnecessary, given the patently reasonable nature of their request. When the others got wind of what they were up to, they were peeved. "Who the hell do they think they are, anyway?" I imagine Peter saying, turning the air blue with expletives of disgust.

We can understand James and John, can't we? True, they lacked discretion, but their instincts were commendable; they had the sort of drive that helps one invent a new technology, or found a successful business, or explore the moon, or win a seat in the Senate. If a new world order was coming, they wanted to be part of it. They wanted to make a difference, to be in positions of influence. Their miscalculation was not realizing how *new* the world order would be; they didn't yet see that everything would be turned upside down.

To the graspers and grumblers, Jesus said, "You know that among the Gentiles those whom they recognize as their rulers lord it over them, and their great ones are tyrants over them. But it is not to be so among you; but whoever wishes to become great among you must be your servant, and whoever wishes to be first among you must be a slave of all. For the Son of Man came not to be served but to serve, and to give his life as a ransom for many."[2]

Jesus didn't upbraid them for their ambition; instead, he showed them how to fulfill it. His advice was counterintuitive: to be great you must become a servant; to be in first place you must head straight for last place.

Not many days later, according to John's Gospel, Jesus demonstrated his point. He and his disciples gathered for their last supper together. Jesus knew that his time of death was near, "that his hour had come to depart from this world and go to the Father," so everything he said and did would be laden with the significance of a farewell. "Knowing that the Father had given all things into his hands, and that he had come from God and was going to God"—this introductory clause is the reason for what follows—he "got up from the table, took off his outer robe, and tied a towel around himself. Then he poured water into a basin and began to wash the disciples' feet and to wipe them with the towel that was tied around him."[3] Precisely because Jesus was the Son of God, the savior of the world, the one unto whom all authority in heaven and earth had been given, the one the church would soon worship as the exalted Lord of the universe, he did the work of a slave. This is the true exaltation, he was saying, the real work of royalty.

The disciples had been walking all day in open sandals, and their feet were sweaty and filthy—unpleasant to imagine, let alone to touch. But Jesus was not too important to do what had to be done. Like the Father who had sent him, Jesus was so exalted he could be humble, so high he could be low; he washed and dried their feet.

After he finished and returned to his place at the table, he said, "Do you know what I have done to you? You call me Teacher and Lord—and you are right, for that is what I am. So if I, your Lord and Teacher, have washed your feet, you also ought to wash one another's feet. For I have set you an example, that you also should do as I have done to you."[4]

{ .. .. }

The story has often been told of German students who, after World War II, volunteered to help rebuild a cathedral in England destroyed in the Luftwaffe bombings. At some point a debate broke out about how best to restore a statue of Jesus with his arms outstretched and bearing the familiar inscription, "Come unto Me." Careful patching could repair everything except the hands, which had been completely destroyed. Should they attempt to reshape those hands? The workers decided to leave the statue with no hands, and the inscription now reads, "Christ has no hands but ours."

Preachers and writers have often used this to illustrate that Christ ministers today through our ministry. This is certainly true, something we should remember. But I'm uncomfortable with the inscription. It implies that Christ would be powerless without our help, unable to get anything done without our cooperation. I find this hard to believe, considering he is the one through whom all things have been created and the one who holds all things together. No, Christ does not depend on the work of our hands; he does not *need* us. But as part of his gift of grace, he chooses to work through our hands; he makes us his partners, his fellow laborers.

Immediately after Jesus told his disciples that they too should wash one another's feet, he said, "If you know these things, you are blessed if you do them."[5] To minister in humility blesses *us;* serving others serves *ourselves.* As foot washers, we learn what lovers and other great givers have always known: those who expend themselves on behalf of others gain more than they ever lose.

Albert Schweitzer was famous as a medical doctor, missionary, musician, biographer, New Testament scholar, and philosopher. He turned his back on wealth and prestige when he sailed for Africa in 1913 and set up his first hospital in an abandoned hen house and made his first operating table out of an old camp bed.

On a trip to the United States, a reporter asked him, "Dr. Schweitzer, have you found happiness in Africa?"

He replied, "I have found a place of service, and that is enough happiness for everyone."[6]

Servants invest time, money, and energy to wash dirty feet, and the investment pays a handsome dividend in happiness. The reason, by now, should be obvious: servants are behaving properly in an upside-down world. Their hands are doing the work of Christ, which means their lives have meaning and purpose; they are part of something much bigger than themselves that will last for eternity.

{ .. .. }

But servants, in my experience, do not have an exalted view of themselves. Most of the time, they simply see that something needs to be done and they get busy doing it. They're not comfortable being called "servant"; in their view, there is nothing sacrificial or heroic about their actions.

Psychiatrist Robert Coles tells about a young man from Birmingham, Alabama, speaking in 1965: "I don't know why I put myself on the line. I don't know why I said no to segregation. I'm just another white Southerner, and I wasn't brought up to love integration! But I was brought up to love Jesus Christ, and when I saw the police of this city use dogs on people, I asked myself what Jesus Christ would [have] thought, and what He would have done—and that's all I know about how I came to be here, on the firing line!"[7]

A disciple of Jesus Christ knows that a world in which barking and biting dogs are set loose on people has to be turned upside down, and the sooner the better. So the disciple acts as though it has already happened, making the problems of Birmingham blacks his own.

Several years ago, I led a weekend retreat for a congregation in the Seattle area. One of the participants was Bruce Kennedy, the former CEO of Alaska Airlines. I was pleased to meet him, having read in the newspaper that he left his position at Alaska Airlines, a position of power and wealth (his 1989 compensation topped $460,000), in order to move to China to teach English to high school teachers. Much of the world didn't understand a decision such as this, but the Kennedys are deeply committed followers of Jesus Christ, and to them it seemed a perfectly reasonable and joyous thing to do. If their Lord can wash dirty feet, it was not a big deal for an important CEO to volunteer his services in China.

Serving, Not Using

For most of us, our serving will not make the newspapers. It consists of helping others, quietly and without fanfare: caring for children, mowing the neighbors' lawn while they're on vacation, taking meals to a friend recovering from surgery, sitting on the church building committee, chairing the local United Way drive, volunteering at the hospital. Nothing dramatic, usually. But there is no such thing as insignificant service in a world of grace, a world where God has come as the Great Servant. All our ministering, whether heroic sacrifice or simple act of kindness, is part of God's grand project of renewing creation; it is imbued with great dignity and eternal meaning.

Chapter Twenty-One

Creating Community, Not Competing

IF WE ARE meant to love, affirm, forgive, and serve others as instruments of God's grace, it's hard to see how competition has much of a place in a world turned upside down. The fundamental rule of competition is that for me to win, you must lose. But if I'm now a partner in Christ's work of serving your best interests, how can I want you to lose?

Of course, it depends on how you define *best.* Many of us, out of Christian charity, would consider it best for the New York Yankees to lose every game, confident that the advancement of much-needed humility would make them better people and the world a happier place. George Steinbrenner, on the other hand, has a different view of the matter. "I want this team to win," he said. "I'm obsessed with winning, with discipline, with achieving. That's what this country is all about."[1]

Unfortunately, he's right: in many ways, that *is* what this country is all about. Our economy thrives on free-market competition, our educational system fosters academic competition, our government runs by political competition, our leisure time enjoys athletic competition, and even our arts and charities depend on fundraising competition. If you want to get ahead in this country—or perhaps I should say, if you want to *survive* in this country—you must throw yourself into the game and compete for all you're worth.

Your worth may be measured by how often you win. I once saw a headline that read, "No Room for Losers at Ohio State." What it meant, of course, is that losers are not welcome, losers have no respect, losers should go to Michigan. But in a world turned upside down by grace, that headline should be abbreviated to "No Losers at Ohio State," for how can there be any losers—at Ohio State or anywhere else in the world—if everyone is a beloved child of God?

I should hasten to add, lest members of my own family toss this book across the room, that I am not suggesting there is anything wrong with baseball. I agree with my friend Matilda, who likes to say that "a double play is a thing of beauty," and I consider a trip to the ballpark, especially if it includes watching the Dodgers get shut out, fine proof of God's existence. Whether or not there will be baseball in heaven, I won't speculate, except to say that if so, in a realm where grace exists in perfection, it will be—somehow, beyond our present understanding—a game that produces no losers, not even for the Dodgers.

My point is simply that where grace reigns, competition ultimately gives way to community. By *community* I mean the mutual serving and bearing of each other's problems and sharing of each other's strengths, which helps make everyone a winner and transforms isolated individuals into a living fellowship.

⁂ .. .. ⁂

Grace, as we have seen, is God's antidote to sin. Our pride, disobedience, and falsehood have caused our hearts to turn in upon themselves (to use Luther's image), thus destroying the harmony of God's original design. Instead of joining in God's dance, we've turned away and done our own silly jig, alone and with no real joy. But grace will not rest until that is changed. So Jesus Christ turns us back toward the center and the Holy Spirit fills us with love for one another, and thus the dance continues. Grace would not be grace, not in its fullest, most radical sense, if we were saved only as individuals and not reshaped into a new community.

Because the essence of sin is pride, grace works toward pride's destruction. Formation of community is God's chief means of accomplishing this end. Community, in other words, is not only a consequence of grace but a *means* of grace, a way in which grace breaks down pride. If you and I are thrown together into a relationship, my pride will conflict with your pride, and something's got to give.

I became a pastor in 1974, a time of racial ferment in many places in our country. My congregation was located in a "transitional" neighborhood, which meant there were many African Americans moving in and many whites moving out. Assuming leadership of a congregation under these circumstances was a witness either to courageous faith or unwarranted self-confidence.

On my first Sunday, a woman I'll call Jane issued a warning: "Pastor," she said, "I want you to know that if you integrate this church, I will oppose you all the way."

A few months later, at the close of a worship service, I suggested that we had to reach out to our community—and fast. The thirty worshipers scattered around the sanctuary could hardly disagree. I asked them to take lists of names and telephone numbers I had prepared and to make a few calls, inviting our neighbors to join us. No one seemed very enthusiastic about doing so, but most were willing to try it.

The following Sunday we were pleasantly surprised to see some newcomers—including our first black family. My excitement over this soon changed to apprehension when I noticed that, of all the possible places in that nearly empty sanctuary, they chose to sit directly behind Jane. I was so worried about what she might say to them I almost skipped the Passing of the Peace when worshippers greeted those near them. But Presbyterians aren't noted for spontaneity; we stick with plans, especially if they've been printed in an Order of Worship. So I had more than a little anxiety as Jane turned around to greet our visitors, and I nearly fainted when she kept talking long after everyone else quieted and I started making the announcements. What was she saying?

Eventually, she turned her attention back to where it belonged—to me—and I proceeded with my sermon, finding it difficult to concentrate on what I was saying while studying the look in her eyes for any clue of what awaited me. Soon after the service, I found out. I took my place at the door, as usual, and Jane came toward me like a runaway freight train.

"Pastor," she said, "did you see those visitors behind me?" (As if I could miss them.) "Well, I . . . I . . ." She sputtered, her face getting red. "I'm the one who telephoned them! I'm the one who invited them!" I couldn't tell whether she was proud or disgusted, and I don't think she knew.

I was smart enough to wait until well after she'd walked away before I laughed. When I did, I had the sense that I wasn't laughing alone; I seemed to hear the sound of a deep laughter filled with the joy of eternity. God knew that Jane had rough edges in need of smoothing, and who better to serve as sandpaper than the very people she didn't like? It was an exquisite gift, one that could only come from a stern but humor-filled grace: Jane herself, without knowing it, had invited the African Americans she so feared but needed to learn to love. The little, flawed community, so weak and uncertain about its future, did something important in her life.

{ .. .. }

Being in community not only challenges us; it strengthens us. Fellowship with others helps us become more than we are by ourselves. God has so created us that we need other people in order to be whole, and so our restoration cannot happen without the community's help. This is the truth, as I understand it, in the much misunderstood doctrine that says there is no salvation apart from the church. A person can have many moving and even ecstatic experiences by himself or herself—with nature, say—but reconciliation with God is not complete apart from reconciliation with the rest of God's children.

This reconciliation happens in many ways; as we love, affirm, forgive, and serve others, we forge relational bonds and community is established. But the primary embodiment of grace-created community is the church, specifically the local congregation. Now, I say this with some reluctance, for I was a pastor for too long not to know that every congregation, no matter how successful it appears from the outside, has its dark side; every one has enough pettiness and conflict and hypocrisy to dispirit the most stalwart member. More than once, I have wanted to get out of the church in order to save my faith. But I've never quite been able to leave, for the simple reason that I cannot. As a follower of Jesus Christ, I have no choice but to remain in the community of Jesus Christ.

In *Turning East,* Harvey Cox documents the impact of Eastern religions on American life, especially student life. At the end of his book, he concludes that Christianity's strength lies in the congregation:

> To grow spiritually, I must apprentice myself to a struggling little church in my neighborhood, a place where I must contend with younger and older people, some of whose views I appreciate and others whose ideas I find intolerable. The music is often stirring, sometimes off key. The preaching is uneven. There is never enough money for the oil, despite numerous potluck suppers. How often have I been tempted to jettison this all-too-human freckle on the Body of Christ and stay home Sunday with better music (on the stereo) and better theology (on the bookshelf). But I do not. A voice within me keeps reminding me

> that I need these fallible human confreres, whose petty complaints never quite overshadow the love and concern underneath. . . . This precious little local church . . . is where the Word becomes flesh. . . . I do not believe any modern Christian . . . can survive without some such grounding in a local congregation.[2]

The church, according to Paul, is the body of Christ, the physical manifestation of Christ's presence on earth. What is a body, if not a unified whole made of complementary parts? Paul strung out this metaphor at some length:

> Indeed the body does not consist of one member but of many. If the foot would say, "Because I am not a hand, I do not belong to the body," that would not make it any less a part of the body. And if the ear would say, "Because I am not an eye, I do not belong to the body," that would not make it any less a part of the body. If the whole body were an eye, where would the hearing be? If the whole body were hearing, where would the sense of smell be? But as it is, God arranged the members in the body, each one of them, as he chose. If all were a single member, where would the body be? As it is, there are many members, yet one body.[3]

The apostle continues to expand on this, becoming redundant and almost beating the life out of the image. An editor would have pruned it back and made it more concise. But Paul wanted to make sure his readers understood that every person has a role in the community of Christ, and only through the community of Christ can every person become whole.

No matter how different you and I may be, no matter how little we have in common, no matter how much we dislike each other, nonetheless we need each other. You have strengths that complement my weaknesses, and vice versa. Only by being together can we become whole. God's grace gives us community, and God's grace uses this community to give us ourselves, to help us become all that we are meant to be.

In that same congregation where June had some of her rough edges knocked off, I had a few of my own chipped away. One day I got crossways with one of the elders; I no longer remember the issue, although I'm certain I was right and he was wrong (at least I remember *knowing* that at the time). I stewed, I agitated, I wondered why God didn't call me to a better church.

Then one night I had a dream: I found a beautiful painting by an "old master," and I was filled with joy, both because it was a magnificent piece of art and because it was worth a great sum of money. Then it occurred to me—the way weird things can in a dream—that I should cut the painting into small squares so I would have more masterpieces. Then I could sell them for even more money! So I found a table saw and turned it on, and I set the painting on the table and began edging it toward the blade. Just as the painting was about to be cut, I awakened. My heart was pounding. I said to myself, "You idiot! You can't cut the painting into pieces. It will only be a masterpiece if it stays together."

That dream was a gift. I wanted to cut the unreasonable elder out of my life, separate myself from him, but God sent a message in the night to remind me that there would be no masterpiece unless we stayed together.

Chapter Twenty-Two

Peace, Not Violence

FOR GAMES AND sports, competition may be appropriate, but as a way of life it has a nasty consequence: it leads to violence. If you must lose for me to win, I'll push you aside to achieve my goals. If you won't get out of my way, I'll have to run over you. If your country must be weak for mine to be strong, we'll threaten with an unsheathed sword. If your country won't meet our demands, we'll have to send in laser-guided bombs.

Is this an unnecessary *reductio ad absurdum?* Well, the absurd is reality: the world is a violent place, and increasingly so. Our coins may declare "In God We Trust," but don't believe it; more than a little evidence suggests that our real hope is in military prowess. The century just ended has been the bloodiest in history, and even a cursory review of it should crush forever any nonsense about the evolution of humanity toward moral goodness.

But establishing community leads to peace. If we need each other—if you must win for me to win—I'll build you up through love, affirmation, forgiveness, and service; I'll have to make room for you, even if it means pushing myself aside for your sake. If your country must be secure for mine to be secure, we'll have to sheathe our swords and learn to wage peace as effectively as we wage war.

"Blessed are the peacemakers," Jesus said, "for they will be called children of God."[1] To be a peace advocate or a peace lover is one thing; to be a peace*maker* is both more difficult and potentially dangerous.

The English word *peace* usually means absence of conflict, connoting something negative. But behind Jesus' teaching stands the great Old Testament word *shalom*. This means more than absence of conflict, connoting something positive. Perhaps the best way to translate it is "wholeness." Biblical peace refers to a comprehensive well-being, a state of completeness. Dale Bruner describes it by using the image of a circle.[2] When the human circle breaks, peacemakers try to complete it; they tie together severed relationships, they reconcile enemies, they heal wounds. Peacemaking isn't simply abolishing warfare; it's creating welfare.

Peacemakers will be blessed, said Jesus, because "they will be called children of God." God is the creator of *shalom*, turning this world's brokenness into wholeness. Through Jesus Christ, "God was pleased to reconcile to himself all things, whether on earth or in heaven, by making peace through the blood of his cross."[3] Even for God, peacemaking is dangerous work. God chose not to get even or to make the guilty pay for their crimes; instead, God chose to suffer human rejection and violence.

In the old world order, peace happened through negotiation or compromise, and sometimes even by destruction (remember the famous comment from the Vietnam War, "We had to destroy the village to save it"?). But this is the world turned upside down by grace: in the new order *shalom* happens through forgiveness that refuses to get even, healing that binds up and salvation that renews.

{ .. .. }

Jesus taught his disciples to adopt God's methods of peacemaking:

> You have heard that it was said, "An eye for an eye and a tooth for a tooth." But I say to you, Do not resist an evildoer. But if anyone strikes you on the right cheek, turn the other also; and if anyone wants to sue you and take your coat, give your cloak as well; and if anyone forces you to go one mile, go also the second mile. Give to everyone who begs of you, and do not refuse anyone who wants to borrow from you.
>
> You have heard that it was said, "You shall love your neighbor and hate your enemy." But I say to you, Love your enemies and pray for those who persecute you, so that you may be children of your Father in heaven; for he makes his sun rise on the evil and on the good, and sends rain on the righteous and on the unrighteous. For if you love those who love you, what reward do you have? Do not even the tax collectors do the same? And if you greet only your brothers and

> sisters, what more are you doing than others? Do not even the Gentiles do the same? Be perfect, therefore, as your heavenly Father is perfect.[4]

These words come from the Sermon on the Mount, the heart of Jesus' teaching. Almost everyone knows that Jesus commanded us to love our enemies, and for many of us this demonstrates that Jesus was a wonderful person—wonderful, but naïve. We wouldn't dream of taking his words seriously. To be sure, we acknowledge love of enemies as the ideal, undoubtedly a fine description of heaven. But a workable ethic for *this* world? Hardly. You can't let people strike you on the cheek without striking back. You have to put fear in the heart of your enemies.

So we simply skip over these verses. We're used to doing this, because we read the Bible selectively, according to our tastes and interests. To illustrate this, let me wander into a highly controversial area: homosexuality. Our culture is deeply divided over this, and the church even more so. Almost every major American denomination is in turmoil over whether to ordain gays and lesbians, as well as whether to bless same-sex unions. This disagreement is not minor; a war is being waged as if the future of Christianity were at stake. On one side are those who uphold biblical authority, and on the other are those who witness to the inclusive love of God—both of which are absolute truths that no one wants to compromise. Hence the conflict.

Now, I'm probably crazy even to introduce this subject, but I'll take the risk to make an observation: the Bible speaks very little about homosexuality. In the New Testament, only Paul refers to it—discussing it briefly in Romans 1, where he lists it, among other things, as a sign of the brokenness of creation. So far as we know, *Jesus never mentioned the subject.*

Why do we eagerly cling to the biblical teaching about homosexuality, taking each word with strict literalness and demanding that others do the same, but at the same time readily ignore what Jesus himself had to say about turning the other cheek and loving our enemies? Well, that's different, isn't it? Jesus must have been speaking about a goal, something for which we should strive—but nothing he actually expected us to do. After all, we live in a dangerous world, and after the tragedy of September 11 we have to be tough, asserting our military muscle to show terrorists and other possible enemies that they had better not provoke us. As I write, we're bogged down in a war of choice, a war we started even though there was no immediate threat to our national security. It was inevitable after September 11, I suppose, because most of us felt we had to do *something,* and bombing a few caves in Afghanistan wasn't enough to satisfy our desire for revenge. So, "praise the Lord and pass the ammunition!"

The truth is, we almost always side with what seems natural. We go with gut instincts—and then we look for biblical support. Condemning homosexuality feels natural because about 95 percent of us could never imagine engaging in such a practice. But loving an enemy feels unnatural, too impossible, because our whole human experience—from rock throwing to missile launching—has been based on the right of self-defense and the use of violence to protect our own interests.

But in a world turned upside down by grace, we must distrust whatever feels natural. God's grace has turned everything on its head, so we should assume that the gut instincts may in fact be nothing but the remains of the old order, and that the ideas that challenge us, even upset us, may in fact be the truth of God's newly emerging reign.

⁂

Am I making a case for pacifism? Am I saying that in a world turned upside down by grace, nonviolence is the only acceptable response to aggression?

Not exactly. To be frank, my own convictions are still a work in progress. I have listened carefully to arguments from those who have argued—often eloquently—for pacifism, and I have engaged in endless debate with others and myself over this matter; I've never been wholly comfortable on one side or the other. The uncertainty of the church as a whole over this is reflected in my own ambivalent convictions. The issue is a knot of theological problems, which I cannot untangle in this brief chapter.

But we can affirm, at least, that the only possible justification for violence is to serve *shalom,* to force establishment of a more just situation. If we are obliged to resort to arms, we must remember two things.

First, the time for conflict is never as soon as we think. The evil we so easily see in the enemy runs straight through every human heart, including our own; we are all sinners, according to Scripture, and given the gravity of God's grace, given the fact that it took the incarnation, death, and resurrection of God's Son to atone for it, we must acknowledge its distorting power. Our judgments will always be flawed and our motives impure; any decision for violence undoubtedly involves our self-interest—often our lust for power, security, or money—and this, moreover, is something we have learned to cloak in lofty ideals and pompous rationalizations.

Second, if we must resort to conflict, we should be honest: we will be disobeying the teaching of Jesus. We may someday find ourselves in a terrible situation in which all our choices are bad; we can't escape the complexities of a broken world. Thus we may—rarely—have no alternative but to resist a wrongdoer. But because this course of action may be less wrong does not make it morally right; sad necessities are not, in themselves, praiseworthy. If we must engage in violence to defend ourselves, we should resist the temptations of self-justification and self-congratulation, and instead we should do what has to be done with humility, repentance, and even a sense of shame, throwing ourselves upon the very grace of God which we, by our actions, are discrediting.

When Dietrich Bonhoeffer, the young theologian killed at the hands of the Nazis, joined the plot to assassinate Hitler, he felt that he was, in a sense, taking sin upon himself. He wondered if he and his colleagues in the conspiracy would be so morally compromised that they would ever again be of use: "We have been silent witnesses of evil deeds; we have been drenched by many storms; we have learnt the arts of equivocation and pretence; experience has made us suspicious of others and kept us from being truthful and open; intolerable conflicts have worn us down and even made us cynical. Are we still of any use?"[5]

The defect of pacifism is that it clings to a principle rather than to Jesus Christ, whose call to obedience sometimes transcends principles. The strength of pacifism is that it clings to a principle taught by Jesus Christ, whose call to obedience most often comes through his command to turn the other cheek and love the enemy.

If we do not struggle with this tension, we have not fully understood that the world has been overturned by grace.

{ .. .. }

To witness to God's grace, however much it might fly in the face of common sense and rational thinking, is the central responsibility of the community of Jesus Christ. Richard B. Hays, professor of New Testament at Duke University Divinity School, has summarized this well:

> One reason that the world finds the New Testament's message of peacemaking and love of enemies incredible is that the church is so massively faithless. On the question of violence, the church is deeply compromised and committed to nationalism, violence, and idolatry. (By comparison, our problems with sexual sin are trivial.) This indictment applies alike to liberation theologies that justify violence against oppressors and to establishment Christianity that continues to play chaplain to the military-industrial complex, citing just war theory and advo-

cating the defense of a particular nation as though that were somehow a Christian value.

Only when the church renounces the way of violence will people see what the Gospel means, because then they will see the way of Jesus reenacted in the church. Whenever God's people give up the predictable ways of violence and self-defense, they are forced to formulate imaginative new responses in particular historical settings, responses as startling as going the second mile to carry the burden of a soldier who had compelled the defenseless follower of Jesus to carry it one mile first. The exact character of these imaginative responses can be worked out only in the life of particular Christian communities; however, their common denominator will be conformity to the example of Jesus, whose own imaginative performance of enemy-love led him to the cross. If we live in obedience to Jesus' command to renounce violence, the church will become the sphere where the future of God's righteousness intersects—and challenges—the present tense of human existence. The meaning of the New Testament's teaching on violence will become evident only in communities of Jesus' followers who embody the costly way of peace.[6]

Chapter Twenty-Three

Stewardship, Not Ownership

THROUGHOUT THIS BOOK, I have been saying that God's grace turns the world upside down, and that it now hangs on the thread of divine mercy—a mercy both revealed and made effective through Jesus Christ. By *world* I mean everything, including the physical universe—from nebulae to newts, from stars to starfish, from black holes to black beetles. The creation came into being through grace; it witnesses to grace and will reach its *telos* (consummation) in grace.

We know this because all things were created through Christ. The Gospel of John tells us that "all things came into being through him, and without him not one thing came into being."[1] Paul tell us that "in him all things in heaven and on earth were created, things visible and invisible, whether thrones or dominions or rulers or powers—all things have been created through him and for him."[2] The author of Hebrews says that God "has spoken to us by a Son, whom he appointed the heir of all things, through whom he created the worlds. . . . He sustains all things by his powerful word."[3] These texts, from diverse sources, indicate that Jesus Christ was not brought into the picture as Plan B, as simply a remedy for the failure of Plan A, but has been eternally one with the Creator and in fact the agent through whom the universe came to exist.

Human sin obliged grace to work in a particular way. Grace had to deal with our pride, disobedience, and falsehood; it needed to heal our brokenness. Because our sin had a ripple effect, grace had more extensive work to do. Paul says that Christ's salvation includes even creation, which "will be set free from its bondage to decay and will obtain the freedom of the glory of the children of God."[4]

Our redemption, in other words, is interwoven with creation's redemption:

> The biblical idea of redemption always includes the earth. Hebrew thought saw an essential unity between man and nature. The prophets do not think of earth as merely the indifferent theater on which man carries out his normal task but as the expression of divine glory. . . . Salvation does not mean escape from bodily, creaturely existence. On the contrary, ultimate redemption will mean the redemption of the whole man. For this reason, the resurrection of the body is an integral part of the biblical hope. The corollary of this is that creation in its entirety must share in the blessings of redemption.[5]

If God has created all things through Jesus Christ, and if grace embraces both us and creation, we are pushed to a significant conclusion: we may not be indifferent to our environment. To put it as bluntly as possible, to despoil creation—polluting oceans, fouling air, decimating forests—is to spit in the face of Jesus Christ, the one through whom all these things have been made. Even as we are to be channels of grace to other people, we are likewise appointed to model God's grace for this earth.

{ .. .. }

Unfortunately, we haven't done this well. Far from treating the earth with grace, we've more often treated it with disgrace. By taming grace and confining it to the realm of individuals, by not understanding that it has turned *everything* upside down, we've often made matters worse.

We're guilty of two things that have exacerbated the problem. First, we've fallen for the ideology of dominion. We can do as we like with the earth, or so we think; we're at the top of the food chain, so why not push our weight around to make the environment serve our purposes? We like being in control (God's place!), and we can even cite a few Bible verses to justify it. At the climax of creation, God said, "Let us make humankind in our image, according to our likeness; and let them have dominion over the fish of the sea, and over the birds of the air, and over the cattle, and over all the wild animals of the earth, and over every creeping thing that creeps upon the earth." So God created humankind, male and female, and said to them, "Be fruitful and multiply, and fill the earth and subdue it."[6]

Primarily because of these verses, the Judeo-Christian tradition has been accused of setting the theoretical foundation for modernity's technocratic manipulation of the environment. On this foundation, much good has been built: a plausible case can be made that, contrary to the pagan worldview, dominion ideology enabled us to transcend creation, to see ourselves as distinct from it, therefore to study it and use it, and thus to invent science. At the same time, however, we've overreached and gone from studying creation to enslaving it, from using it to abusing it.

We've too often neglected the core of Scripture (Jesus Christ) and emphasized the edges (the creation story). But biblical interpretation should move from the center outward, from the living Word outward to the written words. Had we remembered that all things were created through and for Jesus Christ, we might have understood better the first chapter of the Bible. Yes, humans were given dominion over the earth. But humans, the story tells us, were made in the image of God. "In our image, according to our likeness" governs the phrase "let them have dominion."

Are we eager to be little gods, lording it over creation? Then let's remember how God lords it over creation: everything was made and is held together through Jesus Christ. That means *God exercises dominion through loving self-sacrifice.* The image of God, remember, was fully revealed in Jesus Christ ("he is the image of the invisible God"[7]). To be true to the image of God, we must model Christ—caring for creation, loving it, even sacrificing ourselves for it. Dominion is redefined in a world turned upside down.

{ .. .. }

The second reason we haven't always been gracious toward the environment is our ideology of escapism. We've too often ignored the implications of Jesus' incarnation, his bodily resurrection, and his return to this earth; we've assumed that God cares only about spiritual things. God's salvation, we've imagined, is a ticket out of this world. "This world is not my home / I'm just a-passing through" says the Gospel chorus. Thus the world can go to hell in a handbasket for all we care.

Why should we worry about depleting the atmosphere's ozone layer, or warming the globe, or destroying rain forests, or killing off other species? We're on our way to heaven! Yes, there is the small matter—hardly worth mentioning—of what we will bequeath to our grandchildren and great-grandchildren, but don't the "signs" indicate that Christ will return soon?

The New Testament surely looks forward to Christ's return, our "blessed hope"; Christians in every generation, beginning with the first, thought his return was imminent. Perhaps it is. But two thousand years of failed predictions should caution against overweening confidence. Whether the consummation of history will happen tomorrow or a thousand years from now, faith in the God of Jesus Christ allows no escapism. "For God so loved the world that he gave his only Son."[8] If God has not turned away from this world, how can we?

A few days before he was hanged at Flossenburg near the German-Czech border, Dietrich Bonhoeffer wrote these words:

> Now for some further thoughts about the Old Testament. Unlike the other oriental religions, the faith of the Old Testament isn't a religion of redemption. It's true that Christianity has always been regarded

as a religion of redemption. But isn't this a cardinal error, which separates Christ from the Old Testament and interprets him on the lines of the myths about redemption? To the objection that a crucial importance is given in the Old Testament to redemption (from Egypt, and later from Babylon—cf.Deutero-Isaiah) it may be answered that the redemptions referred to here are *historical,* i.e. on *this* side of death, whereas everywhere else the myths about redemption are concerned to overcome the barrier of death. Israel is delivered out of Egypt so that it may live before God as God's people on *earth.* The redemption myths try unhistorically to find an eternity after death. Sheol and Hades are no metaphysical constructions, but images which imply that the "past," while it still exists, has only a shadowy existence in the present.

The decisive factor is said to be that in Christianity the hope for resurrection is proclaimed, and that that means the emergence of a genuine religion of redemption, the main emphasis now being on the far side of the boundary drawn by death. But it seems to me that this is just where the mistake and the danger lie. Redemption now means redemption from cares, distress, and longings, from sin and death, in a better world beyond the grave. But is this really the essential character of the proclamation of Christ in the gospels and by Paul? I should say it is not. The difference between the Christian hope of

> resurrection and the mythological hope is that the former sends a man back to his life on earth in a wholly new way which is even more sharply defined than it is in the Old Testament. The Christian, unlike the devotees of the redemption myths, has no last line of escape available from earthly tasks and difficulties into the eternal. . . . This world must not be prematurely written off.[9]

It is not fanciful to imagine that as Bonhoeffer penned these words the Nazis were tying the knot in his noose. He was hours away from his death—at the age of thirty-nine! He had every right to console himself with thoughts about redemption into a better world beyond the grave. Instead, he challenged his fellow Christians not to abandon this world but to love it as God loves it.

{ .. .. }

Ideologies of dominion and escapism should be replaced with a theology of stewardship. Douglas John Hall is correct: the steward is "a biblical symbol come of age."[10]

What is a steward? For some, the word carries a load of negative baggage; it conjures images of a "stewardship campaign"—the dreaded effort to meet the church budget by challenging parishioners to give more money. It brings to mind endless committee meetings, guilt-producing sermons, and even home visitations to ask for a "pledge." Every church says that stewardship has to do with more than money; each intends to stress the need to give time and talents as well. But no one is ever fooled. The real interest is money, and for this reason *stewardship* has become a four-letter word.

We would do well to recover the biblical understanding. In the Old Testament, a steward is a servant, but not an ordinary one who simply takes orders from others. Rather, a steward is "a sort of supervisor or foreman, who must make decisions, give orders, and take charge. . . . That is, the steward is one who has been given the responsibility for the management and service of something belonging to another, and his office presupposes a particular kind of trust on the part of the owner or master."[11]

Clearly, this is the idea behind the New Testament notion of stewardship. Jesus asked his disciples, "Who then is the wise and prudent manager whom his master will put in charge of his slaves, to give them their allowance of food at the proper time?" The answer, of course, is the one who takes good care of his master's property. Only an incredibly unwise and immensely imprudent manager would, when his master is gone, work out his frustrations by beating the slaves to within an inch of their lives, and then, when tired of swinging the whip, raid his master's cupboard and wine cellar. This would not be good stewardship. If the master returns and sees bloodied slaves and emptied bottles of the Chateau Lafite Rothschild he had been saving for his daughter's wedding, he will not be happy. He will make sure the manager has a hangover from hell, throwing him out with the unfaithful and giving him a severe beating. Jesus concluded this parable by saying, "From everyone to whom much has been given, much will be required; and from the one to whom much has been entrusted, even more will be demanded."[12]

Can anyone doubt that we are those to whom much has been given? We have been blessed, as the apostle says, "with every spiritual blessing in the heavenly places."[13] But because this comes to us "in Christ"—the Incarnate One—the blessing includes the earthly places as well. We have not been given the earth to own, as though it were ours to do with as we please. The words of the psalmist remain true: "The earth is the Lord's and all that is in it."[14] But we have been given it in trust, as a manifestation of grace, and we now have responsibility for it.

When the Master returns, what will he find? Will we have abused the earth to satisfy our insatiable cravings? Will we have depleted its resources and undermined its ability to sustain human life? Or will we tend well what has been placed in our safekeeping? Will we care for what the Master cares for?

Listen to Father Zossima's admonition in *The Brothers Karamazov:* "Brothers . . . love all God's creation, the whole and every grain of sand in it. Love every leaf, every ray of God's light. Love the animals, love the plants, love everything. If you love everything, you will perceive the divine mystery in things. Once you perceive it, you will begin to comprehend it better every day. And you will come at last to love the whole world with an all-embracing love."[15]

Good stewards come at last to love the whole world with an all-embracing love, because they know that's the sort of love their Master has—for them, and for every grain of sand, every leaf, and every ray of light.

Chapter Twenty-Four

Hope, Not Despair

ONE MORNING DURING a trip to the African country of Malawi, I climbed to the top of a nearby mountain. As I sat on a rock, enjoying the view and thanking God for the beauty of creation, I heard faint sounds in the distance. Was the air so clear that I was hearing people in the village below? No; the voices seemed to be getting louder. A group of young people were coming up the mountain. As they got closer, I heard beautiful voices singing a lilting melody and complex harmony. They were praising God, repeating over and over again this phrase: "We have come this far by the mercy of God."

Indeed. They were singing for you and me too, and this whole world. We have come this far by the mercy of God.

But now this question: *Where are we going?*

Why has our world been turned upside down? What does grace intend for us? What will be the outcome of this great upheaval of mercy?

{ .. .. }

To catch a glimpse—it can be only a glimpse—of where we are going, let's start in our own hearts and follow the trajectory of grace into the cosmos.

There is a place deep in the center of each of us where there is no singing. In it can be heard only the sighs of longing. Perhaps it is a part of us that still doubts, or perhaps it is a part that has not yet experienced the joy of grace. But—I think this is most likely—perhaps it is a part of us that is experiencing God's mercy in a painful but growth-producing way. The place itself, strange to say, is a gift of grace.

It's not easy to describe this place, but it manifests itself through an inner restlessness, an unsatisfied longing, a constant agitation toward . . . what? We can't say exactly, except we know it is toward *something else.* This confuses us, especially after believing the good news of Christ. If we have already received the most important spiritual and earthly blessings, why do we have this persistent, gnawing hunger for more? Why do we find ourselves always wishing for a deeper joy, a greater fulfillment, a final satisfaction that grants us peace?

The novelist Reynolds Price says this longing is for "credible news that our lives proceed in order toward a pattern which, if tragic here and now, is ultimately pleasing in the mind of a god who sees a totality and *at last* enacts His will. We crave nothing less than perfect story; and while we chatter or listen all our lives in a din of craving—jokes, anecdotes, novels, dreams, films, plays, songs, half the words of our days—we are satisfied only by the one short tale we feel to be true."[1]

By "perfect story" Price means, I think, a tying up of loose ends into a complete knot, a fitting of jagged-edged pieces into a meaningful picture, a fusing of scattered confusions into a purposeful pattern. We not only want this, we need it. Although God has objectively canceled our sin, we still live with the subjective consequences of it; to be human is to suffer emptiness and even pain. No matter how furiously we perform our own little dance, we find no satisfaction because it cannot replace the larger dance of creation.

So we need more, and *wanting* more is actually a gift from God. Dissatisfaction drives us forward to what might be; it can fill us with hope. Too often, though, we are easily distracted. As C. S. Lewis put it, "If we consider the unblushing promises of reward and the staggering nature of the rewards promised in the Gospels, it would seem that Our Lord finds our desires not too strong, but too weak. We are half-hearted creatures, fooling about with drink and sex and ambition, when infinite joy is offered to us, like an ignorant child who wants to go on making mud pies in a slum because he cannot imagine what is meant by the offer of a holiday at the sea. We are far too easily pleased."[2]

Restlessness can create problems for us, misdirecting our desires to things and experiences that, however entertaining, cannot satisfy. But it can also, by the working of God's grace, fill us with hope for something larger than we ever imagined, something that will yield enduring fulfillment.

Jesus taught us to pray, "Thy Kingdom come, they will be done," because whether or not we know it that's what we really want. We crave the consummation of God's love; we're homesick for heaven. C. S. Lewis said he wondered if, in our heart of hearts, we have ever desired anything else: "All the things that have deeply possessed your soul have been but hints of it—tantalizing glimpses, promises never quite fulfilled, echoes that died away just as they caught your ear. But if it should really become manifest—if there ever came an echo that did not die away but swelled into the sound itself—you would know it."[3]

{ .. .. }

The unanimous witness of the New Testament writers is that the echoes will one day swell into the sound itself, that the consummation of God's love will transform the universe. The resurrection of Jesus promises the victory of salvation and life. This victory is not yet evident; all around us we see sin and death, signs of the old order. But disciples of Jesus have always looked forward to the day when he returns to complete his work and bring to fulfillment God's reign. The last words of Jesus in the Bible are these: "Surely I am coming soon."[4]

Christians differ on the details of what will happen. Bestsellers describe scintillating and sometimes scary scenarios. Truth to tell, most of them should be taken with a grain of salt. No one really knows how the story will end. Scripture offers hints, to be sure, but most often they come to us in highly imaginative language that aims to cultivate confidence rather than delineate doctrine or prerecord history.

What we do know is this: *grace will triumph.* God's salvation will finish its benevolent business, and the renewal of creation will no longer be a dream but an experience. Therefore we have hope, not despair—hope for ourselves, our families, our nation, the world, the cosmos.

The longing in our little hearts leads us toward the immense creation, and our vision is flooded with the all-encompassing light of God.

{ .. .. }

Grace moves from the particular to the universal. God chose Abraham and promised to bless him with many descendents. Although the childless Abraham might have understandably focused on his own good news (he would have a son!), the promise also declared that through him "all the families of the earth shall be blessed."[5] The reason for calling one man, the reason for delivering his descendents from Egyptian slavery and enduring their ungrateful disobedience, the reason for punishing them with Babylonian exile and returning them to Jerusalem, the reason for sending them prophet after prophet, the reason for finally sending the Messiah—the Christ—and the reason for Christ commissioning his disciples to be his witnesses "in Jerusalem, in all Judea and Samaria, and to the ends of the earth"[6]—the reason for *all* God's work in the history of salvation was for *all the families of the earth to be blessed.*

But people of faith have a history of forgetting this. They prefer to feel special, to imagine that they are better than others. They've always had trouble accepting God's gracious intentions for the whole world.

Take Jonah, for example. Some have said his story, however improbable, is historical fact; some have made a case for it being an ancient morality play or piece of short fiction. Whatever its literary classification, it was included in the collection of authoritative texts for God's people. So it's important to listen carefully to it.

God called Jonah to be a preacher. If he was like most of his colleagues, he was hoping for an appointment in a leafy suburb of Jerusalem, preferably a congregation that would have no trouble meeting its budget and taking good care of him. But no such luck. God sent him to Nineveh, of all places, the capital of Assyria, the country that had destroyed Israel with an ancient form of ethnic cleansing. It was a nasty place, nowhere you'd want to preach. So Jonah boarded a boat sailing in the opposite direction, and that's where the whale comes into the story. After the sailors figured out that their troubles began the day they met Jonah, they threw him overboard, whereupon he made a fine dinner for a whale that happened to be swimming by.

That got Jonah serious about his prayer life. He pleaded for help, of course, the way we all do when we're in a whale of problem. God was merciful, as you might expect, afflicting the whale with a gastric problem that got Jonah spewed out onto dry ground. The reluctant preacher had learned his lesson, so with seaweed hanging from his ears he headed for Nineveh to announce the coming judgment.

He had barely concluded his first sermon before a revival broke out. Everyone in the city, including the king, repented and donned sackcloth and started fasting. In fact, the king decreed that even the animals had to fast and be covered in sackcloth.

Now, it can be disconcerting for a preacher when people actually do what he says, and Jonah wasn't happy about it. He knew that if the Ninevites repented, God would forgive them. That was the sort of deity he was working for—one liable to get sentimental. God would just overlook all their rotten behavior and forget they had terrorized the nations around them, that they were disgusting, awful, mean, and ruthless.

Sure enough, *God* repented too and decided not to lower the boom. Jonah was so angry at this turn of events that he threw a huge tantrum. Why should grace extend all the way to Assyria? Whatever happened to *justice?* Jonah pouted and carried on, and God tried to explain the situation by asking him a question: "Should I not be concerned about Nineveh, that great city, in which there are more than a hundred and twenty thousand persons who do not know their right hand from their left, and also many animals?"[7] God seemed to be saying, "Jonah, these people are so stupid I *have* to be kind to them, and besides, look at all these animals running around in *sackcloth!* How can I not be merciful?" If we're not laughing at the end of this story, we may be slower than the Ninevites.

Lest I be accused of picking on only a Jewish preacher, let me be quick to add that the biggest fight in the New Testament era was whether the Gospel should be preached to the Gentiles. Some of the early church leaders fiercely contended that Jesus had come to save only Jews; others, like Peter and Paul, after they had been dragged kicking and screaming to the truth, realized that even Gentiles were included in the embrace of grace. Peter had to be knocked upside the head with a vision that made him see—*forced* him to accept—that God intended to save even those who were ceremonially unclean. Paul had to be knocked to the ground with a vision of the resurrected Christ, and when he started preaching he had to get kicked out of synagogues and even stoned before he decided it was time to preach to Gentiles.

It has never been easy for us to include others in the circle of mercy. Perhaps we like the feeling of being the favored ones; perhaps it makes us feel more secure when we see ourselves on the inside and others on the outside. But grace is always up to something bigger than we imagine; its reach is always more extensive than we suppose. The trajectory of Scripture, we should understand, moves toward universal salvation.

{ .. .. }

Does this mean that everyone will be saved?

Some theologians have made this argument, among them Origen, an early church father, who said that the final restitution would include everything, even the devils. Many ordinary Christians have cherished this hope. Others, however, point to the undeniable fact that the Bible speaks of an eternal death and warns of fearful consequences for unbelief.

Both sides have scriptural support. The Bible is not a textbook of systematic theology. It's really a collection of writings, most of which were written to *do* something in the lives of readers, to stimulate faith or engender obedience or build confidence. Much of our theology therefore must emerge from a negotiated balance between texts, some of which contradict one another. Consequently, deciding on doctrine is messy work, filled with more uncertainties than you'd realize from the dogmatic manner of some Christians.

Actually, the New Testament has two streams of tradition. On the one hand, there is a clear warning that unbelief, turning away from God's love in Christ, leads to eternal death. "Do not fear those who kill the body but cannot kill the soul; rather fear him who can destroy both soul and body in hell."[8] "If your hand causes you to stumble, cut it off; it is better for you to enter life maimed than to have two hands and to go to hell, to the unquenchable fire."[9] Those who do not obey the gospel "will suffer the punishment of eternal destruction, separated from the presence of the Lord and from the glory of his might."[10] These and other passages leave us with the impression that we should not even *think* about not believing.

On the other hand, parts of the New Testament witness to a salvation as wide as the universe. They come from the "highest" passages, where Paul in particular takes an eagle-eye view and writes systematically about the person and work of Christ: "Therefore just as one man's trespass led to condemnation for all, so one man's act of righteousness leads to justification and life for all."[11] "For God has imprisoned all in disobedience so that he may be merciful to all."[12] "With all wisdom and insight he has made known to us the mystery of his will, according to his good pleasure that he set forth in Christ, as a plan for the fullness of time, to gather up all things in him, things in heaven and things on earth."[13] "For in him [Christ] the fullness of God was pleased to dwell, and through him God was pleased to reconcile to himself all things, whether on earth or in heaven, by making peace through the blood of his cross."[14] These and other passages seem to indicate that nothing will finally be excluded from God's grace.

What do we make of this apparent contradiction? The warnings of hell should sober us. It matters—eternally!—what we believe, and we must invite our fellow humans to join us in trusting God's grace in Christ. We ought never to take grace for granted; it is always a surprising gift. Thus the hope of universal salvation should not be hardened into a tenet of theology. Speaking of Origen's belief in universal restoration, Charles Williams said, "It is impossible that some such dream should not linger in any courteous mind, but to teach it as a doctrine almost always ends in the denial of free-will. If God has character, if man has choice, an everlasting rejecting of God by man must be admitted as a possibility; that is, Hell must remain. The situation of the devils (if any) is not man's business. The charity of Origen schematized then too far; he declared as a doctrine what can only remain as a desire."[15]

But surely, as Williams admits, universal salvation may remain a desire—even, on the basis of important New Testament texts, a hope that need not be whispered in secret but shouted in public.

Frederick Buechner tells about signing his first book contract, the fulfillment of his wildest dreams of literary glory. As he left the offices of Alfred Knopf in New York, he seemed to be on the brink of fame and fortune. But what he remembers most from that day was running into someone he had known slightly in college. The other young man was working as a messenger boy. Buechner says that

> instead of feeling pride or accomplishment by the comparison, I remember a great and unheralded rush of something like sadness, almost like shame. I had been very lucky, and he had not been very lucky, and the pleasure that I might have taken in what had happened to me was all but lost in the realization that nothing comparable, as far as I could see, had happened to him. . . . All I can say now is that something small but unforgettable happened inside me as the result of that chance meeting—some small flickering out of the truth that, in the long run, there can be no real joy for anybody until there is joy finally for all of us.[16]

Buechner's feelings were more than the sentiments of a courteous mind (to use Williams's phrase); they were an expression of hope—a Christian hope based on the very love of God that gives reason to believe that one day there will be joy for all.

Many years ago, I decided that I would rather risk erring on the side of God's grace, if that were possible, since mistakes of generosity are likely not considered mistakes in the mind of God. In the Bible, the indisputable movement of God's salvation is toward inclusion rather than exclusion, and we have it on the authority of that same Bible that "all things" (not some things, not many things, not even a majority of things, but *all* things) have been reconciled to God.

Hope, Not Despair

This means, it seems to me, that we can focus our eyes on the most distant horizon and know that God is busy there too, with a good, healing, joy-creating, life-granting work.

{ .. .. }

What will be the final outcome of grace? We don't know exactly, as I've said, but perhaps artists of the imagination—poets and novelists—can help us hear an echo of the music that will one day swell into the sound itself.

In *The Divine Comedy,* Dante tells of his descent into hell and his journey up through purgatory and finally into paradise. As he approaches heaven, he stops to listen to a sound he has never heard before. He writes, "It sounded like the laughter of the universe."[17] This is the laughter of God, as sorrow becomes joy, as death itself dies and love triumphs over all.

At the end of his famous *Chronicles of Narnia,* C. S. Lewis has Aslan, the Christ figure in his stories, tell the children:

> "Your father and mother and all of you are—as you used to call it in the Shadow-Lands—dead. The term is over: the holidays have begun. The dream is ended: this is the morning."
>
> And as He spoke He no longer looked to them like a lion; but the things that began to happen after that were so great and beautiful that I cannot write them. And for us this is the end of all the stories, and we can most truly say that they all lived happily every after. But for them it was only the beginning of the real story. All their life in this world and all their

> adventures in Narnia had only been the cover and the title page: now at last they were beginning Chapter One of the Great Story, which no one on earth has read: which goes on for ever: in which every chapter is better than the one before.[18]

Or best of all, the Revelation to John. When the Holy Spirit opened the eyes and ears of John's imagination, he saw the new Jerusalem, coming down out of heaven from God, prepared as a bride adorned for her husband, and he heard a loud voice from the throne saying:

> See, the home of God is among mortals.
> He will dwell with them as their God;
> they will be his peoples,
> and God himself will be with them;
> he will wipe every tear from their eyes.
> Death will be no more;
> mourning and crying and pain will be no more,
> for the first things have passed away.[19]

Chapter Twenty-Five

Therefore Bear Witness

HOW, THEN, DO we live in an upside-down world?

With astonishment. Lack of astonishment indicates that something is terribly wrong, that somehow we've missed the startling news of God's love for the world (including us). Mike Yaconelli put it this way: "The most critical issue facing Christians is not abortion, pornography, the disintegration of the family, moral absolutes, MTV, drugs, racism, sexuality and school prayer. The critical issue today is dullness. We have lost astonishment. The Good News is no longer Good, it is OK News. Christianity is no longer life changing, it is life enhancing. Jesus doesn't change people into wild-eyed radicals anymore, he changes us into 'nice people.' "[1]

In many churches, the atmosphere is more funereal than celebratory, more routine than startling, more weary than playful. What accounts for such dullness?

It happens when we defend ourselves against grace. We have a natural resistance to it, as I've said; we don't like the disorientation it causes. So we tame it, enshrining it in dusty creeds and sentimental hymns, thus drain it of meaning. That's how Christianity came to be a safe religion, a kind of halfway house where we get a dose of spirituality to make us nice people and help us be more successful in the world, overlooking the fact that this very world has actually been upended. We carry on as though nothing has changed: God is still in heaven, we're still working our way out of guilt, and the world is still divided between those who are in (us) and those who are out (others)—the precise formula for aching dullness.

How do we recover a sense of astonishment? By telling the Story, again and again, to ourselves, to one another, to the whole world; by announcing the good news without moderation and dilution, in all its wonder.

When we *really* hear the news of a world turned upside down, we'll likely have our breath taken away by the catastrophe of it; but we'll realize it's a *good* catastrophe, what J.R.R. Tolkien called "eucatastrophe." A scene from his famous trilogy, *The Lord of the Rings,* shows what this is like:

> [Sam says] "Gandalf! I thought you were dead! But then I thought I was dead myself. Is everything sad going to come untrue? What happened to the world?"
>
> "A great Shadow has departed," said Gandalf, and then he laughed, and the sound was like music, or like water in a parched land; and as he listened the thought came to him that he had not heard laughter, the pure sound of merriment, for days upon days without count.

> It fell upon his ears like the echo of all the joys he had ever known. But he himself burst into tears. Then, as a sweet rain will pass down a wind of spring and the sun will shine out the clearer, his tears ceased, and his laughter welled up, and laughing he sprang from his bed.
>
> "How do I feel?" he cried. "Well, I don't know how to say it. I feel, I feel"—he waved his arms in the air—"I feel like spring after winter, the sun on the leaves; and like trumpets and harps and all the songs I have ever heard!"[2]

We thought we were dead, although we had no idea how dead we were until we were raised from the grave, and then we discovered that life has defeated death. Grace has overturned the world of sin, and now we're in the middle of a eucatastrophe. It's almost impossible not to jump up laughing and express our joy. Something deep within us wants out, and so we speak, or sing, or preach, or chant, or write—*we bear witness.*

This is what we've been commissioned to do, after all. "You will be my witnesses," Christ said.[3] This is a command, not unlike telling my grandchildren "You will eat your ice cream," or a new bride "You will love your husband." Duty and delight are one.

We bear witness, not because it's a new law we must perform, not because we want a bargaining chip for divine favors, but for one reason: gratitude. "Grace and gratitude belong together like Heaven and earth," said Karl Barth. "Grace evokes gratitude like the voice of an echo. Gratitude follows grace like thunder and lightning."

{ .. .. }

We bear witness as we live according to the values of the Great Inversion—as we love, affirm, forgive, serve, create community, wage peace, tend the environment, and surround the world with our hope. Sometimes we do it more explicit ways, as perhaps when we speak as a "joyful partisan of the good God."[4]

My friend Art was a barber before his retirement. For decades he cut hair in the town where I was a pastor. Whenever I tried to tell him to take a bit more off the top or to leave more on the sideburns, he'd say, "Do I tell you how to preach?" Then he would cut as he pleased, completely disregarding my requests, which was usually fine because he was a pretty good barber.

But he was a better witness to Jesus Christ. Every day people sat in his chair, unloading problems on him, telling him about affairs, divorces, bankruptcies, and illnesses. He would listen and promise to pray for them, and sometimes, when it seemed appropriate, he would tell them about Jesus Christ. He never forced his faith down anyone's throat, but simply offered it as part of the conversation—good news that he wanted to share. Some of his customers he invited to a weekly Bible study in his home. Drug addicts and doctors were there, as well as surfers and bankers, teachers and carpenters; it was always an eclectic group. They gathered for one reason: to tell and hear the Story, to name the grace that they first felt in Art's concern and later learned was part of God's.

Sitting in Art's chair, you could rarely get through a haircut without his being interrupted by a skateboarder stopping to say hello, or a businessman calling to report how his wife was doing with her cancer, or a mom introducing her kid to "the man who cut Grandpa's hair." A few months ago I walked with Art down the street, and I was slightly annoyed at having to stop every three minutes so people could talk with him. I wondered whether I, in my big-deal pastorate, preaching to hundreds of people every Sunday, was even half as effective as Art in communicating the love of God. There is no artifice in Art; he's simply astonished and grateful for God's grace, and so he naturally talks about it and demonstrates it through his care for others.

As I lift my eyes from my computer screen, I see a print of a painting by Matthias Grünewald, the center panel of his Isenheim altarpiece, *Christus am Kreuz.* I read about this picture thirty years ago in a biography of Karl Barth. He greatly admired the painting, which made me want to see it. I searched everywhere to find a print for myself, eventually ordering one from Germany. When it finally arrived, I hung it within sight of my desk; it has remained near my desk in five studies for nearly three decades.

In the center of the picture is Christ on the cross. He is, without doubt, the *suffering* servant. His body is not what you'd see in a painting by Rubens, say, but more like what you'd see in a movie by Mel Gibson: beat up, disfigured, almost inhuman. The crossbeam, to which his hands are nailed, is curved, as if each end is bent downward by the weight of the world's sin. In the lower right corner of the picture is John the Baptist. He's pointing to Jesus. His forearm and hand are proportionally too large, especially the elongated finger, and they are bright against a black background. Grünewald wants us to pay attention to the pointing finger.

That's what we do at the foot of the cross: we point to the humiliation of God and the glory of humanity, to the truth of who God is and who we are. We have no interest in grace as an abstract idea. We know only this God-Man hanging in love, and we know him because he's also the Living One who has commissioned us to be his disciples in this upside-down world.

Notes

Chapter One

1. Barth, K. *Church Dogmatics* (vol. IV/3/1, G. W. Bromiley, trans.). Edinburgh, Scotland: T. and T. Clark, 1961, p. 259.

Chapter Two

1. Capon, R. F. *The Parables of Judgment.* Grand Rapids, Mich.: Eerdmans, 1989, p. 53.
2. Matthew 20:16. All scriptural quotations are from the New Revised Standard Version unless otherwise noted.
3. Chesterton, G. K. *St. Francis of Assisi.* Garden City, N.Y.: Image Books, 1957, pp. 74–75.
4. Chesterton (1957), p. 78.

Chapter Three

1. Dillard, A. *Teaching a Stone to Talk.* New York: HarperCollins, 1982, p. 40.
2. Revelation 8:1.

Chapter Four

1. Mark 3:1–6.
2. Genesis 3:3–11.
3. Romans 8:31–32, 38–39.
4. Miller, A. *Timebends.* New York: HarperCollins, 1987, p. 482.

Chapter Five

1. John 1:1.
2. John 1:14.
3. My understanding of God's grace is greatly indebted to Karl Barth, especially the magisterial fourth volume of his *Church Dogmatics* (which includes five thick books!). He argued that sin consists of pride, disobedience, and falsehood, and that we know this because we see its opposite in Jesus Christ. Jesus Christ was both the Son of God who humbled himself for our sake and the Son of Man who was obedient in our place, and as both God and Man he is the Truth that dispels the darkness of our falsehood.
4. Milton, J. "On the Morning of Christ's Nativity." In A. W. Allison and others (eds.), *The Norton Anthology of Poetry* (rev. ed.). New York: Norton, 1975, pp. 310–311.
5. I John 1:1; 4:2.
6. I Corinthians 10:31.

Chapter Six

1. Matthew 1:23.
2. Mark 15:34.
3. Romans 5:18.
4. Colossians 1:20.
5. Colossians 1:15.
6. I Corinthians 1:23–29.
7. Matthew 5:3.
8. Buick, S. M. *Parables.* Oct. 1990, p. 4.

Chapter Seven

1. Mankoff, R. *New Yorker,* Dec. 22 and 29, 2003.
2. I Corinthians 15:20–22.

3. I Corinthians 15:23–24.
4. John 10:10.
5. Buechner, F. *Whistling in the Dark: An ABC Theologized.* San Francisco: HarperSanFrancisco, 1988, p. 42.

Chapter Eight

1. Hebrews 1:1–3.
2. Colossians 2:9.
3. Ephesians 1:4.
4. I John 4:8, 16.
5. As quoted by Willimon, W. "Love in Action." In J. W. Cox and K. M. Cox (eds.), *Best Sermons* (3rd ed.). New York: HarperCollins, 1990, p. 205.
6. Isaiah 54:7–8.
7. Hebrews 12:5–11.
8. Heschel, A. J. *The Prophets* (vol. 2). New York: HarperCollins, 1962, p. 4.
9. Heschel (1962).
10. Manning, B. *Lion and Lamb: The Relentless Tenderness of Jesus.* Old Tappan, N.J.: Chosen Books, 1986, pp. 96–97.

Chapter Nine

1. Ephesians 2:4–9.
2. Hebrews 11.
3. Jude 3.
4. James 2:19.
5. Ephesians 2:8–9.

Chapter Ten

1. Romans 7:15.
2. See Smedes, L. B. *Shame and Grace.* San Francisco: HarperSanFrancisco, 1993, p. 9.

3. Timpe, R. L. "Shame." In D. G. Benner (ed.), *Baker Encyclopedia of Psychology.* Grand Rapids, Mich.: Baker Book House, 1985, p. 1075.
4. John 8:1–11.

Chapter Eleven

1. Romans 6:23.
2. Romans 3:23.
3. John 3:16.
4. De Pree, M. *Dear Zoe.* San Francisco: HarperSanFrancisco, 1996, p. 28.
5. Mark 8:34–35.
6. Buechner, F. *Wishful Thinking: A Theological ABC.* New York: HarperCollins, 1973, p. 41.
7. Luke 7:11–17.
8. Mark 5:35–43.
9. John 11:1–44.
10. II Corinthians 5:17.
11. John 11:25.

Chapter Twelve

1. Becker, E. *The Denial of Death.* New York: Free Press, 1973.
2. II Corinthians 1:8–9.
3. Capon, R. F. *The Foolishness of Preaching: Proclaiming the Gospel Against the Wisdom of the World.* Grand Rapids, Mich.: Eerdmans, 1998, pp. 26–27.
4. Bob has told his story in *Heaven's Back Row: From Homosexuality and HIV to Hope and a New Beginning.* Irvine, Calif.: Spirit of Hope, 2003.

Chapter Thirteen

1. Becker (1973), pp. 283–284.

2. Peck, M. S. *The Road Less Traveled: A New Psychology of Love, Traditional Values, and Spiritual Growth.* New York: Simon & Schuster, 1978, p. 50.

Chapter Fourteen

1. Baillie, D. *God Was in Christ.* New York: Scribner, 1948, p. 205.
2. Psalm 40:8.
3. Psalm 119:14, 16, 24, 143, 174.

Chapter Fifteen

1. Clapp, R. "Why the Devil Takes Visa." *Christianity Today,* Oct. 7, 1996, p. 20.
2. Luke 12:15.
3. Luke 12:16–19
4. Ephesians 1:3–5.
5. As quoted in Cavanaugh, B. *The Sower's Seeds.* Mahwah, N.J.: Paulist Press, 1990, pp. 47–48.
6. Wakefield, D. *Returning.* New York: Doubleday, 1988, p. 178.
7. I first told this story in my book *Say Please, Say Thank You: The Respect We Owe One Another.* New York: Putnam, 1998, pp. 134–135.
8. Luke 6:38.
9. Lewis, C. S. "The Weight of Glory." In *The Weight of Glory and Other Addresses.* New York: Macmillan, 1980, p. 4.

Chapter Sixteen

1. Dillard (1982), p. 20.
2. Kazantzakis, N. *Christ Recrucified.* London: Faber and Faber, 1962, pp. 186–187.

3. As quoted in "From the Lectionary." *Preaching*, Jan./Feb. 1994, p. 56.
4. John 19:30.
5. I am indebted to the late Bruce W. Thielmann for these final words. Many years ago, I heard them in a sermon of his, and I'm pleased to acknowledge my gratitude for his remarkable preaching ministry.
6. John 17:4.

Chapter Seventeen

1. Owens, V. S. *And the Trees Clap Their Hands.* Grand Rapids, Mich.: Eerdmans, 1983, p. 4.
2. Owens (1983), p. v.
3. Owens (1983), p. 1.
4. Matthew 22:37–40.
5. John 13:34–35.
6. Barth, K. *Church Dogmatics* (vol. IV, part II, Bromiley and Torrance, eds.). Edinburgh, Scotland: T. and T. Clark, 1958, pp. 819–820.
7. II Corinthians 3:18.
8. Galatians 5:22.
9. Selzer, R. *Mortal Lessons.* New York: Simon & Schuster, 1974, pp. 45–46.

Chapter Eighteen

1. Romans 5:15, 17–18.
2. Singer, J. *Boundaries of the Soul: The Practice of Jung's Psychology.* New York: Doubleday, 1972, p. 165.
3. Tucker, C. "Family Values Sinner Is Exposed." *San Francisco Chronicle,* June 19, 1999, p. A20.
4. Matthew 7:3.

5. John 3:16–17.
6. I told this story in my book *The Wisdom of Pelicans: A Search for Healing at the Water's Edge.* New York: Viking Compass, 2002, p. 98.

Chapter Nineteen

1. Bruner, F. D. *The Christbook: A Historical/Theological Commentary—Matthew 1–12.* Waco, Tex.: Word Books, 1987, p. 251.
2. Luke 23:34.
3. Capon, R. F. *The Parables of Grace.* Grand Rapids, Mich.: Eerdmans, 1988, p. 47.
4. Luke 18:21–35.
5. Tillich, P. *The New Being.* Magnolia, Mass.: Peter Smith, 1955, pp. 7–8.
6. Kelsey, M. *Reaching.* New York: HarperCollins, 1989, p. 113.
7. Guinness, O. "More Victimized Than Thou." In O. Guinness and J. Seel (eds.), *No God but God.* Chicago: Moody, 1992, p. 92.
8. Acts 7:60.
9. Arnold, J. C. *Seventy Times Seven.* Farmington, Penn.: Plough, 1997, p. 31.
10. Manning (1986), pp. 135–136.

Chapter Twenty

1. Mark 10:33–34.
2. Mark 10:42–45.
3. John 13:3–5.
4. John 13:13–14.
5. John 13:17.

6. As quoted in *Parables, Etc.*, Nov. 1989, 9(9), 5.
7. Coles, R. *Harvard Diary: Reflections on the Sacred and Secular.* New York: Crossroad, 1988, pp. 23–24.

Chapter Twenty-One

1. As quoted in *Sales Upbeat, 100*(4).
2. Cox, H. *Turning East: The Promise and Peril of the New Orientalism.* New York: Simon & Schuster, 1977, p. 174.
3. I Corinthians 12:14–20.

Chapter Twenty-Two

1. Matthew 5:9.
2. Bruner (1987), p. 149.
3. Colossians 1:20.
4. Matthew 5:38–48.
5. Bonhoeffer, D. *Letters and Papers from Prison* (E. Bethge, ed.). London: SCM Press, 1971, p. 16.
6. Hays, R. B. *The Moral Vision of the New Testament: Community, Cross, New Creation; A Contemporary Introduction to New Testament Ethics.* San Francisco: HarperSanFrancisco, 1996, pp. 343–344.

Chapter Twenty-Three

1. John 1:3.
2. Colossians 1:16.
3. Hebrews 1:3.
4. Romans 8:22.
5. Ladd, G. E. *Jesus and the Kingdom: The Eschatology of Biblical Realism.* New York: HarperCollins, 1964, pp. 55, 59.
6. Genesis 1:26, 28.

7. Colossians 1:15.
8. John 3:16.
9. Bonhoeffer (1971), pp. 119–120.
10. Hall, D. J. *The Steward: A Biblical Symbol Come of Age.* Grand Rapids, Mich., and New York: Eerdmans, 1990.
11. Hall (1990), p. 32.
12. Luke 12:42–48.
13. Ephesians 1:3.
14. Psalm 24:1.
15. Dostoyevsky, F. *The Brothers Karamazov* (C. Garnett, trans.). London: Heinemann, 1912, p. 332.

Chapter Twenty-Four

1. As quoted in Peterson, E. H. *Answering God: The Psalms as Tools for Prayer.* San Francisco: HarperSanFrancisco, 1989, p. 45.
2. Lewis (1980), p. 3.
3. Lewis, C. S. *The Problem of Pain.* San Francisco: HarperSanFrancisco, 2001, pp. 150–151.
4. Revelation 22:20.
5. Genesis 12:3.
6. Acts 1:8.
7. Jonah 4:11.
8. Matthew 10:28.
9. Mark 9:42.
10. II Thessalonians 1:9.
11. Romans 5:18.
12. Romans 11:32.
13. Ephesians 1:9–10.
14. Colossians 1:19–20.

15. Williams, C. *The Descent of the Dove.* Grand Rapids, Mich.: Eerdmans, 1939, p. 40.
16. Buechner, F. *The Sacred Journey.* San Francisco: HarperSanFrancisco, 1982, p. 97.
17. As quoted in Rosenberger, D. "Fear Vanquished." In M. Duduit (ed.), *Great Preaching 1991.* Nashville, Tenn.: Abingdon Press (Preaching Resources), 1991, pp. 22–23.
18. Lewis, C. S. *The Last Battle.* New York: HarperTrophy, 1956, 1984, pp. 210–211.
19. Revelation 21:2–4.

Chapter Twenty-Five

1. Yaconelli, M. *Dangerous Wonder.* Colorado Springs: NavPress, 1998, p. 16.
2. Tolkien, J.R.R. *The Lord of the Rings.* Vol. 3: *The Return of the King.* New York: Ballantine Books, 1970, p. 283.
3. Acts 1:8.
4. Busch, E. *Karl Barth* (J. Bowden, trans.). Philadelphia: Fortress Press, 1976, p. 408.